THE TOP 100 HEALING FOODS

THE TOP 100 HEALING FOODS

PAULA BARTIMEUS

DUNCAN BAIRD PUBLISHERS

LONDON

THE TOP 100 HEALING FOODS

Paula Bartimeus

For Sri Chinmoy, my spiritual teacher who for many, many years has molded and enriched my life beyond my imagination. Although he no longer resides on the earth plane, his presence is felt all-where and he shall eternally remain my inner and outer guide.

Distributed in the USA and Canada by Sterling Publishing Co., Inc., 387 Park Avenue South New York, NY 10016-8810

This edition first published in the UK and USA in 2009 by Duncan Baird Publishers Ltd, Sixth Floor, Castle House, 75–76 Wells Street, London W1T 3QH

Library of Congress Cataloging-in-Publication Data
The top 100 healing foods : 100 foods to relieve ailments and enhance health and vitality / Paula Bartimeus.
    p. cm.
  Includes bibliographical references and index.
  ISBN 978-1-84483-731-1 (alk. paper)
 1. Diet therapy--Handbooks, manuals, etc. 2. Nutrition--Handbooks, manuals, etc. 3. Natural foods--Handbooks, manuals, etc. I. Title. II. Title: Top one hundred healing foods.
  RM217.2.B37 2009
  615.8'54--dc22

                    2008042841

10 9 8 7 6 5 4

Typeset in Helvetica Condensed
Color reproduction by Colourscan, Singapore
Printed in Malaysia for Imago

Publisher's Note: The information in this book is not intended as a substitute for professional medical advice and treatment. If you are pregnant or breastfeeding or have any special dietary requirements, allergies, or medical conditions, it is recommended that you consult a medical professional before following any of the information or recipes contained in this book. Duncan Baird Publishers, or any other persons who have been involved in working on this publication, cannot accept responsibility for any errors or omissions, inadvertent or not, that may be found in the recipes or text, nor for any problems that may arise as a result of preparing one of these recipes or following the advice contained in this work.

Notes on the recipes
Unless otherwise stated: • Use fresh herbs • Use large eggs • 1 tsp. = 5ml, 1 tbsp. = 15ml, 1 cup = 240ml

For information about custom editions, special sales, premium and corporate purchases, please contact Sterling Special Sales Department at 800-805-5489 or specialsales@sterlingpub.com.

CONTENTS

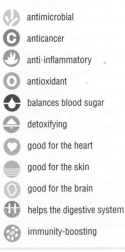

KEY TO SYMBOLS

- antimicrobial
- anticancer
- anti-inflammatory
- antioxidant
- balances blood sugar
- detoxifying
- good for the heart
- good for the skin
- good for the brain
- helps the digestive system
- immunity-boosting

introduction

"Let food be thy medicine and medicine be thy food."

HIPPOCRATES

Our ancestors knew well the healing power of natural foods and turned to them to combat all sorts of maladies. It's only now, centuries later, that research has begun to confirm that the therapeutic benefits of these foods can be scientifically proven. In fact, some foods have been found to work even better than drugs —and without the adverse side effects.

From apples and almonds to honey and brown rice, this handbook will help you to get to know the many amazing medicinal properties found in everyday foods and learn which ones are useful for particular ailments. These top 100 healing foods not only prevent a wide range of health problems but help to alleviate them as well. And note that nearly all these foods are available from your local supermarket or healthfood store, apart from one or two ingredients which you may need to locate in a more specialized store. Mind you, you'll know they are worth finding when you realize the difference to your health—and hence to your life—such foods can make!

Most experts now agree that eating a diet rich in natural, health-giving foods can help us to ward off common complaints such as colds, coughs, and infections as well as to protect ourselves against chronic degenerative diseases, including cancer, heart disease, and arthritis. So, next time you're feeling below par, instead of turning to the medicine cabinet, turn to your own fridge or kitchen cupboard where, with the help of this great book, you're likely to find a remedy.

To make the book easy to use, the carefully selected 100 wonderfoods have been divided into six main, color-coded sections: Vegetables; Fruit; Grains, Beans, and Legumes; Nuts and Seeds; Herbs and Spices; and Others, which includes an assortment of interesting food items. Each food entry offers practical and reliable information, along with a simple delicious recipe suggestion, a nutrient list, and at-a-glance symbols highlighting its key healing properties. In addition, there are ten star foods that are especially highlighted for their remarkable health secrets and each of these includes two recipes. Finally, at the back of the book, you'll find an ailments directory for easy reference.

FOODS THAT HEAL
VEGETABLES
If there's one food group we can never eat too much of, it has to be vegetables. Abundant in vitamins, minerals, fiber, and water, vegetables help to cleanse and alkalize the body, neutralizing acidity and reducing the toxic load. They are also low in fat and calories (with the exception of starchy vegetables, such as potatoes, taro, winter squash and yams) and are one of the best sources of phytochemicals—potent plant compounds that help to protect the body against disease.

Scientific research suggests that phytochemicals slow down the aging process and reduce the risk of diseases and health concerns, including cancer, heart disease, high blood pressure, cataracts, osteoporosis, and arthritis. Most of them function as antioxidants, helping to counteract the hazardous effects of free radicals—unstable molecules that damage body cells. In fact, free radical damage is thought to be one of the main causes of aging. Phytochemicals exert various other mechanisms, such as stimulating the immune system, regulating hormones, and providing antibacterial and antiviral activity. The great news is that all vegetables are brimming with these natural plant components, of which hundreds have now been identified.

Try to make vegetables a central feature of main meals and find new ways of incorporating them into your diet, so that you eat generous amounts every day. When preparing salads,

instead of sticking to basic ingredients like lettuce, cucumber, tomatoes, and carrots, use them only as a base, and add a variety of other colorful ingredients such as celery, red bell pepper, radicchio, beet, fennel, watercress and daikon. Cooked vegetables are good too, especially in the winter. To preserve fragile nutrients such as vitamin C, steam, stir-fry, or bake them rather than boil them, or add them to soups and stews. Juicing is another great way of reaping the goodness from vegetables in a more concentrated form.

FRUIT

Generally fruit contains more vitamins than vegetables, whereas vegetables rate higher in the mineral stakes. Most fruits are exceptionally cleansing and alkalizing, helping to eliminate toxins from the body and to regulate the digestive system by stimulating movement of the digestive tract and improving the body's ability to absorb nutrients. Fruits are also a fantastic source of enzymes, natural sugars, and cell-protective phytochemicals.

As the body digests fruits relatively quickly (within 30 minutes), they are best eaten on their own, separately from other foods that take longer to digest. This prevents them from fermenting in the digestive tract. Between meals is probably a good time to fit them in, unless you opt for an all-fruit breakfast.

Both fresh and dried fruits are nutrient-rich, with dried fruits also being an excellent source of minerals. While freshly pressed fruit juices are good for you, it's advisable to dilute them with water to reduce their fruit-sugar content. This will help to curb blood sugar fluctuations and lower the calorie count, which can add up when fruits are juiced, as well as reduce the risk of dental caries.

STORAGE TIPS

• Most vegetables should be stored in the fridge to help slow down their deterioration. It's best not to wash or chop them up until ready to use as they have a natural protective coating that helps to keep them fresh. Mushrooms are best stored refrigerated in paper bags. Don't refrigerate garlic, onions, winter squash, and potatoes—they can be left uncovered in a cool dark place and eaten within a week or so.

• With the exception of berries, grapes, fresh figs, melons, and pineapple, most fruit can be stored at room temperature until ripe. To speed up ripening, place fruit in a closed paper bag out of direct sunlight.

• Store grains, beans, and legumes in airtight containers in a cupboard and label them with their use-by date. Once cooked, they will keep in the fridge for up to three days. Cooked beans can also be frozen.

• Unrefined vegetable oils are best kept in the fridge with the exception of olive oil, which solidifies unless kept at room temperature. Unrefined oils turn rancid quickly when exposed to heat and light.

• Nuts, seeds, and their butters also contain oils and should be kept refrigerated to prevent them from going rancid.

• Fresh herbs can be preserved by placing their stems in small water-filled glass jars and covering them with plastic wrap. They should then be refrigerated. Keep dried herbs and spices in clean, dry glass jars with airtight lids and store them away from light and heat to prevent loss of flavor.

GRAINS

Grains are the primary source of energy for many people throughout the world. Unrefined grains are rich in slow-releasing carbohydrates that help sustain and fuel the body. They are also rich in fiber to aid digestion.

There are two main types of fiber— soluble and insoluble. Soluble fiber helps to stabilize blood sugar levels and to lower high cholesterol, while insoluble fiber regulates bowel movements. Grains contain both types.

Some grains, such as quinoa and amaranth, provide the body with complete protein; other grains need to be combined with beans, legumes, or seeds to make their protein more usable by the body. This can easily be achieved and we often do it automatically when preparing meals in traditional combinations—

for example, in beans on toast, rice and dal, rice with chili beans, and so on.

Like fruit and vegetables, grains have many healing vitamins, minerals, and phytochemicals. Most grains supply B-vitamins, needed for normal metabolism and a healthy nervous system, along with calcium and magnesium and various trace elements.

If you are allergic or intolerant to gluten (a sticky protein found in wheat, rye, barley, and oats), there are plenty of grains which are gluten-free, such as rice, millet, buckwheat, quinoa, and amaranth.

BEANS AND LEGUMES

Beans and dried legume seeds (often simply called legumes) are an excellent source of protein—especially when combined with grains—as well as soluble and insoluble fiber and complex carbohydrates. This makes them ideal energy foods for balanced blood sugar. They also contain a broad spectrum of minerals and a brain nutrient called lecithin. If legumes cause you to bloat, their gassy effects can be avoided by adding a few bay leaves or a strip of kombu seaweed during the cooking process.

NUTS AND SEEDS

Both these food groups provide protein, minerals, and vitamin E, which are very important for the skin, reproductive organs, and circulatory system. They are also packed with the healthy fats associated with lowering high cholesterol, balancing hormones, and reducing inflammation. The high fat content of nuts and seeds means they are calorie-laden, so eat them in moderation. They are ideal sprinkled on salads, cereals, and desserts, or as snacks. Also, nut and seed butters make tasty spreads on toast or crackers.

HERBS AND SPICES

Besides adding taste and aroma, herbs and spices boost the nutrient content of all kinds of meals. They also make fabulous substitutes for salt and some aid the digestive process.

To preserve the nutrients and flavor of both fresh and dried herbs, add them to dishes toward the end of the cooking time. However, it's best to add spices earlier to allow their flavor to develop fully. As well as being a real treat for our taste buds, herbs and spices can be made into medicinal teas (see box, above) to help to relieve various health problems.

HOW TO MAKE A MEDICINAL TEA

Place scant ½ cup fresh herbs or heaping 1 tablespoon dried herbs or spices in a saucepan, pour 2½ cups of boiling water over them, and cover. Let steep 10 to 15 minutes, then strain. For coarser parts of the herb, such as stems, roots, and barks or for spices, simmer the ingredients for 20 minutes to allow the goodness to be released. Infusions will last up to three days in the fridge and should be drunk two to three times a day.

OTHERS

There are some foods that do not fit into any of the categories mentioned so far, but without which no book on healing foods would be complete. These include protein-rich items, such as turkey, salmon, eggs, and live yogurt; condiments, such as apple cider vinegar, which has long been valued as a curative; and natural sweeteners such as honey, carob, blackstrap molasses, and xylitol. In some cases, such as dark chocolate, scientific research has only recently verified its array of healing benefits.

Additionally, a few Oriental treasures, such as miso, umeboshi, and kuzu, have been included because of their exceptional medicinal and culinary uses.

USEFUL INFORMATION

• All recipes have been designed to serve four, although quantities may vary according to the size of the portion required.

• Always opt for organic food wherever possible. Organic produce is believed to contain more nutrients than intensively farmed food, and is free from potentially harmful chemicals.

• In an age when food allergies and intolerances are becoming increasingly prevalent, the saying "one man's meat is another man's poison" is absolutely accurate. So just because a particular food is endowed with therapeutic properties, do not assume that you will not react to it. Remember that it can still make you feel unwell if you are sensitive to it. If you suspect that you are reacting to certain foods, it is wise to get a comprehensive food allergy test.

Common food allergies include meat, fish, dairy, eggs, soy, wheat, gluten, nuts, and yeast, although any food can be potentially problematic.

• Some healing foods possess naturally-occurring toxins, such as goitrogens and oxalic acid, which may aggravate specific health conditions. Fortunately, most of these compounds are deactivated during cooking. However, potatoes, tomatoes, eggplants, and bell peppers contain substances called solanines that may exacerbate arthritis, as can citrus fruit.

C 🤚 ◎ 🔺 ≡

cucumber

NUTRIENTS
Vitamins B3, B5, C, K, beta-carotene, biotin, folate; calcium, iodine, iron, magnesium, manganese, phosphorus, potassium, silica, zinc

The high water and mineral content of cucumber is largely responsible for its therapeutic cleansing and hydrating effects.

The expression "cool as a cucumber" is probably founded upon this vegetable's extremely high water content, which gives it refreshing and cooling qualities. Cucumber is a good source of the mineral silica, a component of connective tissue found in the skin. This, coupled with cucumber's large percentage of water, helps to keep skin cells well-nourished and hydrated. Cucumber can also be used topically to relieve various skin afflictions, including puffy eyes and sunburn. The vitamin C and caffeic acid in cucumber, which relieve inflammation and water retention, may explain why it is so effective for the skin.

GARDEN SALAD

2 large handfuls baby spinach leaves
1 cucumber, chopped
8 radishes, trimmed and thinly sliced
2 scallions, peeled and thinly sliced
1 spring onion, trimmed and chopped
2 tbsp. chopped parsley
1 tbsp. olive oil
juice of ½ lime

Combine the vegetables and parsley in a large bowl. Pour the olive oil and lime juice over them, and toss well. Serve immediately.

tomato

Bursting with vitamin C, tomatoes are also packed with lycopene, one of the most potent cancer-fighting phytochemicals.

The exceptional feature of tomatoes is their high concentration of lycopene, a carotenoid compound which gives them their bright red color. A higher intake of lycopene in the diet has been associated with a reduced risk of several cancers, including those of the prostate, lung, and stomach. It has also been found to protect the skin from sun damage. Tomatoes are rich in potassium, which regulates fluid balance, and are an excellent source of vitamin C, which boosts the immune system.

NUTRIENTS
Vitamins B3, B5, B6, C, E, K, beta-carotene, biotin, folate; calcium, iodine, iron, magnesium, manganese, phosphorus, potassium, zinc; fiber

Cooking tomatoes increases their lycopene availability and anticancer properties.

TOMATO RAITA

30 cherry tomatoes
1¾ cups plain live yogurt
1 scallion, trimmed and finely chopped
1 tbsp. finely chopped cilantro leaves
1 tbsp. finely chopped mint
½ tsp. roasted ground cumin sea salt to taste

Cut the tomatoes into quarters, place them in a baking tray and broil until slightly soft. Let cool, then transfer to a bowl. Add the yogurt, scallion, cilantro, mint, cumin, and salt. Mix well and serve as a dip.

003

red bell pepper

NUTRIENTS
Vitamins B3, B6, C, E, K,
beta-carotene, biotin, folate;
calcium, iodine, iron, magnesium,
manganese, phosphorus,
potassium, zinc; fiber

The wide range of nutrients in this colorful vegetable make it a great all-round immunity-booster.

Red bell peppers have a high water content, which helps to flush out toxins from the body. They are also packed with vitamin C and beta-carotene, useful for warding off colds and infections, and fortifying the immune system. One 5-ounce serving contains an average person's daily needs of these vitamins. Like tomatoes, red peppers are one of the few foods containing lycopene, an antioxidant with anticancer properties.

RED PEPPER SAUCE

2 red bell peppers, seeded
  and chopped
2 cups cashews
1 tsp. freeze-dried dill
1 clove garlic
1 tbsp. chopped onion
pinch of black pepper

Put all the ingredients in a
food processor and blend until
creamy. Serve over grains or
steamed vegetables or use as
a sandwich spread.

fennel

This pale green bulb is packed with disease-preventing antioxidants and can be eaten either raw or cooked.

Fennel is a natural diuretic and promotes health in the liver, kidneys, and spleen. Like many vegetables, it contains phytochemicals, including rutin, quercetin, and kaempferol, which all act as powerful antioxidants. Rutin strengthens blood capillaries, thereby improving poor circulation, while quercetin inhibits inflammatory conditions such as asthma. Kaempferol has been found to reduce heart disease risk. Anethole, another compound in fennel, is anti-spasmodic, preventing the intestinal spasms often experienced by people with irritable bowel syndrome.

NUTRIENTS
Vitamins B3, B5, C, E, K, beta-carotene, biotin, folate; calcium, iodine, iron, magnesium, manganese, phosphorus, potassium, selenium, zinc; fiber

SAUTÉED FENNEL

1 tbsp. olive oil
2 fennel bulbs, trimmed and finely sliced
8 cloves garlic
ground black pepper

Heat the oil in a pan, add the fennel, and gently fry the garlic until slightly soft. Season with black pepper. Serve as an accompaniment or with some crusty wholegrain bread and cheese.

celery

NUTRIENTS
Vitamins B3, B5, C, E, K,
biotin, folate; calcium, iodine,
iron, magnesium, manganese,
molybdenum, phosphorus,
potassium, selenium, sodium,
zinc; fiber

Containing concentrates of many amazing therapeutic compounds, just three celery stalks make up one of the five recommended daily portions of fruit and vegetables.

Vital minerals can be lost in the sweat following vigorous exercise or during a fever. Celery juice, with its high concentration of water, potassium, and naturally-occurring sodium, can help to replace this loss by hydrating the body and restoring electrolyte balance. As celery juice has a strong flavor, it is best mixed with other juices, such as carrot.

Celery leaves can be cut off and used for flavoring soups and salads.

CLASSIC WALDORF SALAD

5 celery stalks, finely chopped
2 apples, chopped
medium bunch white seedless
   grapes
1 scallion, trimmed and
   chopped
a handful chopped walnuts
2 tbsp. mayonnaise
2 tbsp. plain live yogurt
½ tsp. celery seeds
ground black pepper, to taste

Put the celery, apples, grapes, scallion, and walnuts in a large bowl. Put the remaining ingredients in a separate small bowl and stir well. Tip the mixture onto the salad and mix well. Serve immediately.

REDUCE STRESS EFFECTS

With its rich mineral content, celery helps to normalize the body's acid–alkaline balance. An acidic state caused by stress or eating harmful foods can lead to numerous health problems. Celery seems to counteract this acidity, thereby improving conditions such as fatigue, rheumatism, and joint pain.

BLOOD PRESSURE BONUS

Besides being a natural diuretic, celery has been found to lower high blood pressure. Compounds called pthalides help to relax the muscles around arteries, allowing blood vessels to dilate. This provides more room for blood to flow, hence lowering the blood pressure. Other healing compounds in celery include coumarins, which enhance the immune system, as well as acetylenics, which have cancer-fighting properties.

CELERY WITH COTTAGE CHEESE AND CHIVES

6 celery stalks
heaping 1 cup cottage cheese
a handful of chopped pecans
1 tbsp. finely chopped chives
ground black pepper, to taste

Cut the celery stalks into generous bite-size lengths. Mix the cottage cheese with the nuts, chives, and pepper, and use it to fill the ribs in the celery stalks. Serve as a light lunch or snack.

leek

NUTRIENTS
Vitamins B1, B3, B5, B6, C, E, K, beta-carotene, biotin, folate; calcium, iodine, iron, magnesium, manganese, phosphorus, potassium, selenium, zinc; fiber

LEEK AND PECAN SAUCE

1 tbsp. olive oil
1 leek, trimmed and chopped
½ cup pecans
1 tsp. ground mustard
1 tsp. wholegrain mustard
scant 1 cup milk or soy milk
heaping 1 tsp. dried thyme
½ tsp. crumbled vegetable
bouillon cube

Heat the oil in a pan and sauté the leek until soft. Then, place it in a food processor along with the remaining ingredients and blend until creamy. Serve either hot or cold on potatoes or other vegetables.

For low cholesterol and a super healthy heart, leeks should be included in the diet on a regular basis.

Leeks are related to garlic and onions, and contain many of the same health-promoting compounds as these vegetables. According to research, they lower total and LDL (bad) cholesterol, increase the HDL (good) cholesterol, and bring down high blood pressure—making them a wonderfood for the heart and circulatory system. Regular consumption of leeks is also associated with a reduced risk of several forms of cancer, while their combination of vitamins and minerals helps to stabilize blood sugar levels.

eggplant

This versatile vegetable protects the brain from aging and may help to keep infections at bay.

Well-known as a main ingredient in the Greek dish moussaka, eggplants contain many beneficial substances including nasunin, an anthocyanin found to protect fats in brain cells from free-radical damage, which may help to slow down the aging process of this vital organ. Another important healing compound found in eggplant is chlorogenic acid, whose potent antiviral, antibacterial, and antifungal properties are thought to aid the body in resisting infections.

NUTRIENTS
Vitamins B3, C, K, biotin, folate, beta-carotene; calcium, iodine, iron, magnesium, manganese, phosphorus, potassium, selenium, zinc; fiber

EGGPLANT GRATIN

2 eggplants
3 tbsp. olive oil
1 cup grated cheddar cheese or dairy-free alternative

Cut the eggplants into slices and brush the sides with the oil. Arrange them in a baking dish in overlapping slices, cover with foil, and cook in a preheated oven at 425°F for 25 minutes. Remove the foil and cook for another 10 minutes. Remove from the oven, sprinkle with the grated cheese, and place under a broiler until the cheese has melted.

asparagus

High in nutrients, low in calories, and rich in flavor, asparagus has many health benefits to offer.

According to folklore, asparagus is considered to be a tonic for the reproductive system. It's an excellent source of folic acid (which protects against neural tube birth defects), and beta-carotene and vitamin C—antioxidant nutrients which help to fight cancer, heart disease, and eye problems. Asparagus also works as a mild diuretic, thanks to its high potassium content and asparagine, an amino acid found in this vegetable. Eating asparagus makes the urine smell quite strongly in some people, but this effect is harmless.

Eat asparagus as soon as possible after purchasing, as it tends to toughen up quickly.

NUTRIENTS

Vitamins B1, B3, B5, C, E, K, beta-carotene, biotin, folate; calcium, iron, magnesium, manganese, phosphorus, potassium, selenium, zinc; fiber

ASPARAGUS, EGG, AND BELL PEPPER SALAD

10 asparagus spears, chopped
1 red bell pepper, seeded and thinly sliced
3 tbsp. olive oil
3 hard-boiled cage-free eggs, shelled and chopped
2 tbsp. chopped chives
2 tbsp. chopped parsley
ground black pepper

Steam the asparagus 8 to10 minutes, then put it in a large bowl. Meanwhile, gently fry the red pepper in 2 tbsp. of the oil until soft, and add it to the asparagus with the eggs, herbs, and remaining oil. Mix gently and season with black pepper.

600

artichoke

This classy vegetable has a special healing affinity with the liver, gallbladder, and digestive system.

Since ancient times, the artichoke has been used as a digestive aid and to ease liver and gallbladder disorders. Its main active constituent is cynarin, a phytochemical which enhances digestion, particularly following meals high in fat. Studies have shown that cynarin reduces nausea, abdominal pain, constipation, and flatulence in people who regularly experience digestive problems. Artichokes may also help to lower high cholesterol levels by inhibiting the production of more cholesterol.

NUTRIENTS
Vitamins B1, B2, B3, B5, B6, C, E, K, beta-carotene; calcium, copper, iron, magnesium, manganese, phosphorus, potassium, selenium, zinc; fiber

---

SPICY ARTICHOKE DRESSING

14 oz. fresh artichokes or
    canned artichoke hearts
2 tbsp. unrefined sunflower oil
1 tbsp. lemon juice
½ clove garlic
1 tsp. mild chili powder
½ cup vegetable juice

If using fresh artichokes, break off the outer leaves and cut away the inner leaves. Scrape out and boil the hearts for about 20 minutes. If using canned artichokes, put all the ingredients in a food processor and blend until creamy.

lettuce

NUTRIENTS
Vitamins B1, B3, B5, C, E, K, beta-carotene, biotin, folate; calcium, iodine, iron, magnesium, manganese, phosphorus, potassium, selenium, silica, zinc

A salad staple, lettuce helps to cleanse the blood, relax the nerves, and eliminate excess fluid.

This leafy vegetable contains a natural sedative called lactucarium, which relaxes the nervous system and induces sleep. To treat insomnia, try drinking lettuce juice before going to bed. With its high potassium content, lettuce is also a mild diuretic, while its chlorophyll helps to detoxify the blood and liver. Other nutrients in lettuce include folic acid, important for preventing birth defects, and beta-carotene and vitamin C, two immunity-boosting vitamins, which help to keep colds at bay.

GREEN SALAD SUPREME

3 large handfuls of mixed
   lettuce leaves
½ cucumber, sliced
scant 1 cup feta cheese, cubed
1 avocado, peeled, pitted, and
   chopped
2 tbsp. alfalfa sprouts
2 tbsp. chopped chives
2 tbsp. olive oil
1 tbsp. cider vinegar
sea salt and ground black
   pepper, to taste

Put all the ingredients in a large bowl, toss well, and serve.

Choose darker colored lettuce varieties over paler-looking ones, as they contain more nutrients.

radicchio

Also known as red chicory, this attractive, red-leaved vegetable adds antioxidant power to salads.

A mainstay in the Mediterranean diet, radicchio has long been praised for its blood-purifying effects. Moreover, it is among some of the highest-scoring vegetables for antioxidant activity. In particular, it is rich in anthocyanins, phytochemicals which help to strengthen blood capillaries and inhibit inflammation, making radicchio a beneficial food for circulatory problems and conditions, such as asthma and arthritis. Additionally, radicchio contains intybin, a mild appetite stimulant, which aids digestion and liver function.

NUTRIENTS

Vitamins B1, B2, B3, B5, B6, C, E, K, beta-carotene, folate; calcium, copper, iron, magnesium, manganese, phosphorus, potassium, selenium, zinc

RADICCHIO WITH BEANS

1 radicchio
a handful of peanuts
1 tbsp. chopped flat-leaf
  (Italian) parsley
¾ cup fine green beans,
  trimmed and chopped
¾ cup fava beans
3 tbsp. olive oil
juice of ½ lemon

Arrange the radicchio leaves in a large bowl with the peanuts and parsley. Steam the green beans for 8 minutes and the fava beans for 20 minutes, then add them to the salad. Mix the oil and lemon juice, pour it over the salad, and toss well.

spinach

NUTRIENTS

Vitamins B3, B5, B6, C, E, K, beta-carotene, biotin, folate; calcium, chromium, iodine, iron, magnesium, manganese, phosphorus, potassium, selenium, sodium, zinc; fiber

This popular type of greens contains a powerhouse of nutrients that protect the body from numerous degenerative diseases.

Containing at least 13 different flavonoid antioxidants, spinach may reduce the risk of heart disease, stroke and several cancers. It is also rich in lutein, a carotenoid compound that helps to guard against age-related eye diseases. Furthermore, spinach is a superb food for the bones, as it provides calcium and magnesium as well as vitamin K, which is thought to play an important role in bone mineralization.

CHEESE AND SPINACH MELT

1 onion, chopped
1 tbsp. olive oil
2 cloves garlic, crushed
heaping ⅓ cup pine nuts
4 cups baby leaf spinach
2⅔ cups grated cheese

Gently fry the onion in the oil, add the garlic and pine nuts, and stir in the spinach until it wilts. Drain off any excess liquid, then add the cheese, stirring until it melts. Use the mixture in crêpes, on toast, or to stuff vegetables.

013

Ⓒ ☙ ◉ ⬖ ♡ ⬎ ⊛

watercress

Packed with more than 15 vitamins and minerals, watercress has long enjoyed superfood status.

Weight for weight, watercress contains more calcium than milk, more iron than spinach, and as much vitamin C as oranges, making it an excellent food for the bones, blood, and immune system. It is also a fabulous source of lutein and zeaxanthin —types of carotenoids that reduce the risk of eye disease. Watercress also possesses a unique compound called PEITC, which has not only been found to inhibit the growth of cancer, but is thought to kill existing cancerous cells as well.

NUTRIENTS
Vitamins B1, B3, B5, B6, C, E, K, beta-carotene, biotin, folate; calcium, iodine, iron, magnesium, manganese, phosphorus, potassium, zinc

CARROT, ORANGE, AND WATERCRESS SALAD

1 bunch watercress, trimmed
2 carrots, peeled and grated
1 orange, peeled and chopped
1 avocado, peeled, pitted, and
    chopped
a handful of walnuts
1 tbsp. chopped oregano
1 tbsp. chopped parsley
2 tbsp. unrefined sunflower oil
juice of ½ lemon
sea salt and ground black pepper

Put the watercress, carrots, orange, avocado, walnuts, and herbs in a large bowl. Add the sunflower oil, lemon juice, salt, and pepper, and toss well. Serve immediately.

okra

NUTRIENTS

Vitamins B1, B3, B5, B6, C, K, beta-carotene, biotin, folate; calcium, iodine, iron, magnesium, manganese, phosphorus, potassium, selenium, zinc; fiber

Also known as lady's finger, okra is high in fiber, helping to regulate bowel function and encourage the growth of friendly bacteria in the gut.

Native to Africa, okra has found its way into many types of global cuisine including Indian, Caribbean, and Middle Eastern cooking. Its main health attribute is its fiber content, which helps to stabilize blood sugar levels and lower high cholesterol, reducing the risk of heart disease. It also has a bulking effect in the large intestine, thereby preventing or alleviating constipation. Okra secretes a mucilaginous juice during cooking, which adds body when used to prepare curries, soups, and sauces.

EASY OKRA

2 tbsp. unrefined sunflower oil
1 onion, chopped
1 tsp. crushed red chilies
1 tsp. ground cumin
1 tsp. turmeric
2 tbsp. tomato paste
12 oz. okra, trimmed and
   chopped

Heat the oil in a pan and gently fry the onion until soft. Add the chilies, cumin, turmeric, and tomato paste, and stir for a minute or so. Add 1¼ cups water and the okra, bring to a boil, and simmer, covered, for about 12 minutes until tender. Serve as a side dish.

shiitake mushroom

This highly-prized mushroom has been revered in the Far East for thousands of years, both as a tasty food and a potent medicine.

Several therapeutic compounds have been identified in shiitake mushrooms. Lentinan not only stimulates the immune system, but appears to trigger the production of interferon, which has antiviral and anticancer properties and is used in Japan to treat cancer, AIDS, diabetes, chronic fatigue syndrome, and fibrocytic breast disease. Eritadenine, another component in shiitake, reduces cholesterol, while tyrosinase lowers blood pressure. Shiitake mushrooms are available either fresh or dried.

NUTRIENTS
Vitamins B1, B2, B3, B5, B6, C; calcium, copper, iron, magnesium, manganese, phosphorus, potassium, selenium, zinc; fiber; protein; omega-6 essential fatty acids

FRIED MUSHROOM SALAD

3 large handfuls of mixed salad greens
1 bunch of watercress, trimmed
4 tbsp. olive oil
1lb. shiitake mushrooms
8 cloves garlic, crushed
ground black pepper

Put the salad greens and watercress in a bowl. Heat 3 tbsp. of the oil in a pan and sauté the mushrooms and garlic until tender. Add the contents of the pan to the salad with the remaining oil. Toss well, season with black pepper, and serve.

avocado

NUTRIENTS
Vitamins B1, B2, B3, B5, B6,
C, E, K, beta-carotene, biotin,
folate; calcium, copper, iodine,
iron, magnesium, manganese,
phosphorus, potassium, zinc; fiber;
monounsaturated fats; lecithin

Contrary to popular belief, avocados can be helpful during a weight-loss program.

Shunned by dieters because of their high calorie count, avocados may actually aid weight loss by satisfying hunger, improving metabolism, and balancing blood sugar levels. Full of health-giving nutrients, they are an excellent source of vitamin E and healthy monounsaturated fats, which help to nourish the skin and protect against stroke and cardiovascular disease. Another type of fat in this delicious, creamy food is lecithin, which plays a role in improving brain function.

AVOCADO DIP

**2 ripe avocados, peeled,
pitted, and chopped
½ onion, chopped
1 clove garlic, crushed
2 tbsp. chopped fresh cilantro
4 tomatoes, chopped
1 green chili, seeded and
chopped
2 tbsp. crème fraîche
1 tbsp. fresh lime juice
pinch of black pepper**

Put all the ingredients in a food processor and blend until creamy. To prevent the dip from going brown, place the avocado pit in it and cover with plastic wrap.

Avocado can be used as a healthy spread in place of butter or margarine.

olive and olive oil

The regular consumption of olive oil in Mediterranean countries could explain the robust health enjoyed by many people who live there.

Rich in vitamin E and monounsaturated fats, olives and their oil have been found to lower high cholesterol, an effect thought to be linked to the phytosterols responsible for reducing cholesterol absorption from food. Olives also contain squalene, which has heart-protecting properties, oleoeuropein, which lowers high blood pressure and oleocanthal, which relieves inflammation. Olive oil can be used to soften wax inside the ears.

Choose "extra virgin" olive oil which contains the most antioxidants and nutrients.

NUTRIENTS

Vitamins E, K, beta-carotene; calcium, copper, iodine, iron, magnesium, manganese, phosphorus, potassium, selenium, zinc; monounsaturated fats

GREEK PASTA SALAD

4 cups wholemeal pasta
3 tomatoes, chopped
½ cucumber, peeled and chopped
1 scallion, trimmed and chopped
¾ cup black olives
scant ½ cup feta cheese or dairy-free alternative, cubed
⅓ cup chopped parsley
3 tbsp. olive oil
sea salt and ground black pepper, to taste

Cook the pasta in boiling water until *al dente*, then drain. Transfer to a large bowl and add all the other ingredients. Mix well and serve.

cabbage

NUTRIENTS
Vitamins B1, B3, B5, B6, C, E, K, U, beta-carotene, biotin, folate; calcium, iodine, iron, magnesium, manganese, phosphorus, potassium, selenium, zinc; fiber

Often overlooked as a healing food, the humble cabbage has much to offer in therapeutic benefits.

FIGHTS CANCER

A member of the cruciferous food family, cabbage contains powerful anticancer compounds, namely indoles and sulforaphane. Recent studies have shown that people who eat at least three servings of cruciferous vegetables each week have a lower risk of prostate, colorectal, and lung cancer. In addition, indoles help to deactivate estrone, a dangerous form of estrogen that is associated with breast cancer.

HEALS ULCERS

A substance unique to raw cabbage known as vitamin U or S-methylmethionine has had remarkable success in healing stomach and duodenal ulcers within as little as four days. Drinking just four glasses of raw cabbage juice every day appears to dramatically reduce the pain and healing time of gastro-intestinal ulcers. The amino acid glutamine, which has anti-inflammatory properties, may also contribute to this.

Cabbage leaves can be used for enhancing the healing process of leg ulcers, wounds, and varicose veins when applied externally to the problem area. Mastitis or breast inflammation,

---

STIR-FRIED CABBAGE WITH LEEKS

2 tbsp. olive oil
½ savoy cabbage, shredded
1 leek, trimmed and chopped
3 cloves garlic, crushed
ground black pepper

Heat the oil in a wok and stir-fry the cabbage, leek, and garlic until cooked through. Season with black pepper and serve as a vegetable side dish.

often experienced by mothers when breast-feeding, may also be relieved in this way.

In addition, cabbage can be a useful aid for gastro-intestinal health—the German fermented cabbage product *sauerkraut* supports the digestive tract by promoting the growth of friendly bacteria in the gut.

SAVOY POTATO CASSEROLE

1 tbsp. olive oil
½ savoy cabbage, shredded
3 large potatoes, peeled and
  cubed
1 tbsp. unhydrogenated
  margarine
sea salt and black pepper

Heat the oil and 2 tbsp. water in a large pan and sauté the cabbage for 8 minutes. Meanwhile, steam the potatoes for 15 minutes, place in a bowl with the margarine, and mash. Add the cabbage, season with salt and pepper, and mix well. Put the mixture in a dish and bake in a preheated 400°F oven for 40 minutes.

broccoli

NUTRIENTS

Vitamins B1, B3, B5, B6, C, E, K, beta-carotene, biotin, folate; calcium, iodine, iron, magnesium, manganese, phosphorus, potassium, zinc; fiber

Touted as a superfood, broccoli is crammed with an amazing blend of nutrients.

A relative of cabbage, broccoli contains potent anticancer compounds including diindolylmethane and sulforaphane, which work together to inhibit cancer growth. Diindolylmethane also promotes antiviral and antibacterial activity, so eating broccoli regularly may help to protect against and fight off infections. Its other health benefits include calcium and magnesium, which promote bone-building; lutein and zeaxanthin, which reduce the risk of eye disease; and vitamin C which fortifies the immune system.

PUREED BROCCOLI SOUP

1 tbsp. olive oil
2 shallots, finely chopped
1 clove garlic, crushed
1 sweet potato, peeled and cubed
1 tomato, chopped
3¼ cups vegetable broth
2 cups chopped broccoli
croutons

Heat the oil in a large pan and gently fry the shallots, garlic, sweet potato, and tomato for a few minutes. Add the broth and broccoli, bring to a boil, and simmer, covered, for 20 minutes. Pour the mixture into a blender and whiz until smooth. Tip back into the pan and heat through. Serve with croutons.

020

carrot

Known for its ability to aid night vision, this root vegetable can be used in both sweet and savory dishes or pressed into a delicious, sweet juice.

Carrots are one of the richest sources of beta-carotene, a carotenoid which is converted into vitamin A in the body. This vitamin is required for normal vision, healthy-looking skin, and effective reproductive function, as well as for helping the body to fight infections such as colds and bronchitis. Eating just two carrots a day appears to reduce high cholesterol levels. This is likely to be due to calcium pectate, a type of soluble fiber that provides them with their characteristic crunchiness.

NUTRIENTS
Vitamins B1, B3, B5, B6, C, E, K, beta-carotene, biotin, folate; calcium, iodine, iron, magnesium, manganese, phosphorus, potassium, selenium, zinc; fiber

CARROT AND CELERY COCKTAIL

10 large carrots, peeled
3 raw beets, peeled
2 celery stalks
2 green peppers, seeded
3½ cups spinach
a large handful of parsley

Cut the carrots, beets, celery and peppers into small chunks and press them through a juicer along with the spinach and parsley. Stir and drink immediately.

Ⓒ Ⓞ ⬆ ⬇ ♥ ≡ ⊕ ⚙

beet

NUTRIENTS
Vitamins B3, B5, C, folate,
beta-carotene; calcium, iodine,
iron, magnesium, manganese,
phosphorus, potassium, zinc; fiber;
carbohydrate

Valued for their powerful detoxifying capabilities, beets are a very effective internal cleanser.

Containing the powerful antioxidant betacyanin, which gives this root vegetable its deep red color, beets help to cleanse the liver, gallbladder and kidneys. Betacyanin also boosts the activity of natural antioxidant enzymes in the body, which protect cells against the dangers of free radical damage. A rich source of natural sugars, beets provide easily digestible carbohydrates for energy, while their dietary fiber content is useful for preventing digestive problems.

RAW BEET SALAD

2 raw beets
½ celeriac
1 carrot
2 tbsp. sunflower seeds
1 tbsp. chopped parsley
2 tbsp. chopped chives
¼ cup plain live yogurt
1 tbsp. olive oil
1 tbsp. lemon juice
sea salt and ground black
    pepper, to taste

Peel and grate the beets, celeriac, and carrot, and put them in a large bowl with the sunflower seeds and fresh herbs. Mix together using your hands. Then, add the remaining ingredients and mix well.

To retain the maximum amount of nutrients and color in beets, peel them after cooking.

Jerusalem artichoke

Sweet and nutty in flavor, Jerusalem artichokes are an excellent source of slow-releasing energy.

Not to be confused with the globe artichoke, the Jerusalem variety is an edible tuber whose brown knobbly appearance resembles ginger root. It's rich in inulin, a type of carbohydrate that does not elevate blood sugar levels, making it a helpful food for diabetics. Inulin also encourages the growth of friendly bacteria in the gut, thereby promoting the health of the digestive tract. Nutrient-wise, this vegetable contains good amounts of iron needed for the formation of red blood cells, while its potassium content provides a mild diuretic effect.

NUTRIENTS
Vitamins B1, B3, C, E, K, beta-carotene; copper, iron, magnesium, manganese, phosphorus, potassium, selenium; fiber; protein; complex carbohydrate

Although the Jerusalem artichoke is related to the sunflower, it grows well in cold climates.

ARTICHOKE FRENCH FRIES

2 lb., 4 oz. Jerusalem
  artichokes
juice of 2 lemons
3 tbsp. olive oil
2 bay leaves
ground black pepper

Cut the artichokes into fries and put them in a roasting tray. Squeeze the lemon juice over them, along with the olive oil. Add the bay leaves to the tray and cook in a preheated oven at 375°F for about 40 minutes until soft and golden. Serve sprinkled with black pepper.

daikon

This mild-flavored, giant white radish cleanses the liver and assists in the digestion of fats.

Daikon, or mooli as it's also called, is a long, white radish popular in Japanese, Chinese, and Korean cuisines. Containing active enzymes, it is often served raw and grated as a side dish to aid the digestion of fatty or oily meals. Daikon also enhances liver detoxification and is said to help to break up catarrh. Being high in water and very low in calories, it's a perfect food for anyone on a weight-loss diet.

NUTRIENTS
Vitamin C; calcium, iron, magnesium, phosphorus, potassium; fiber

ORIENTAL COLESLAW

1 daikon, trimmed and peeled
3 carrots, peeled
½ white baby cabbage
2 scallions, trimmed and chopped
1 tbsp. gomasio (optional)
2 tbsp. toasted sesame oil
1 tbsp. rice vinegar
sea salt, and ground black pepper

Grate the daikon, carrots, and cabbage and put them in a large bowl. Add the remaining ingredients and mix well. Serve with noodles and a protein source such as fish or tofu.

taro

High in complex carbohydrates and low in fat, taro makes a tasty change to rice or potatoes.

Also known as eddo and dasheen, taro is a small, tropical root vegetable with a mild, nutty flavor. High in complex carbohydrates, it is an excellent energy food and offers a delicious alternative to potatoes but with a lower glycemic index. It is also a good source of potassium, which gives it a mild diuretic action. Once peeled, taro can be boiled, steamed, or roasted, as well as added to soups and casseroles.

NUTRIENTS
Vitamins B1, B3, B5, B6, C, E, K, beta-carotene, folate; calcium, copper, iron, magnesium, manganese, phosphorus, potassium, selenium, zinc; fiber; protein; complex carbohydrate

ROASTED CHILI TARO

4 taro, peeled
3 tbsp. olive oil
1 tsp. chili powder

Cut the taro into chunks and steam them for about 5 minutes. Transfer them to a roasting tray and sprinkle with the oil and chili powder. Roast in a preheated 425°F oven for 30 minutes, turning them half-way through the cooking time.

C 🖐 ⊙ ♥ ✺

potato

NUTRIENTS
Vitamins B1, B3, B5, B6, C, K, biotin, folate; calcium, iodine, iron, magnesium, manganese, phosphorus, potassium, selenium, zinc; fiber; protein; complex carbohydrate

The world's premier vegetable crop, potatoes are inexpensive, versatile, and packed with health-giving nutrients.

Often shunned for their high carbohydrate content, potatoes are fattening only if fried or covered in butter. A good all-round source of nutrition, they contain B-vitamins needed for metabolism, potassium which helps to regulate the elimination of fluid, and vitamin C, which boosts immunity. They also possess flavonoids, known for their anticancer and anti-inflammatory properties, as well as compounds called kukoamines, which lower blood pressure.

SCALLOPED POTATOES

4 potatoes, peeled and sliced
2 tbsp. olive oil
sea salt, and ground black
   pepper
scant 1 cup vegetable broth

Brush the potato slices with the oil, season and arrange in a casserole dish with the slices overlapping. Pour broth over them, cover with foil and cook in a preheated 425°F oven for 1 hour. Then remove the foil and cook for an extra 15 minutes or until the liquid has evaporated.

sweet potato

From soups, casseroles, and salads to baby food and desserts, sweet potatoes add taste, valuable nutrients, and color to any meal.

Orange-fleshed sweet potatoes are probably best known for their rich concentration of beta-carotene, which is converted into vitamin A in the body. This nutrient plays an important role in vision, bone growth, reproduction, and keeping the lining of the digestive and respiratory tracts healthy. Sweet potatoes are also low in fat and loaded with potassium, which helps to maintain fluid balance in cells. Despite the name "sweet," this vegetable contains blood-sugar-regulating properties and is considered to be a useful food for diabetics.

NUTRIENTS
Vitamins B1, B3, B5, C, E, beta-carotene, biotin, folate; calcium, iodine, iron, magnesium, manganese, phosphorus, potassium, selenium, zinc; fiber; protein; complex carbohydrate

---

MASHED SWEET POTATO

4 sweet potatoes, peeled and chopped
3 carrots, peeled and chopped
1¼ cups frozen peas
2 tbsp. butter or unhydrogenated margarine
sea salt and ground black pepper

Steam the sweet potatoes, carrots, and peas 20 to 25 minutes until soft. Transfer to a bowl, add the butter or margarine, and salt and pepper, and mash until creamy. Serve instead of mashed regular potatoes.

027

Ⓒ Ⓞ ⬆ ♡

yam

An excellent power food, yam is a delicious and sustaining form of slow-releasing carbohydrate.

Used in a similar way to potatoes, yams have a lower glycemic index and so provide a more sustained form of energy. This makes them a good source of carbohydrate for diabetics and weight-watchers. Yams are high in potassium and low in sodium, which helps to regulate fluid balance. Their vitamin C and B6 content and dietary fiber all contribute to good health.

YAM VEGETABLE STEW

2 tbsp. olive oil
1 onion, chopped
1 clove garlic, crushed
½ yam, peeled and chopped
2 carrots, peeled and chopped
1 zucchini, chopped
2 celery stalks, chopped
1 tsp. paprika
1¼ cups vegetable broth
1 tbsp. chopped parsley

Heat the oil in a pan and gently fry the onion. Add the garlic, vegetables, and paprika, and stir for 2 minutes. Add the broth, bring to a boil and simmer, covered, for 15 minutes. Add the parsley just before serving.

horseradish

Used as a medicine in the Middle Ages, horseradish has antibacterial, diuretic, and stimulant properties.

The kick and aroma of horseradish are almost unnoticeable until it is cut or grated and its volatile oils are released. These oils, particularly mustard oil, have natural antibiotic properties that can help to treat various ailments, including respiratory tract infections such as coughs and sinus congestion, and urinary tract infections. This root vegetable stimulates the digestion and is an effective diuretic. It also promotes perspiration, making it useful for cold and flu relief.

NUTRIENTS
Vitamins B3, C, K, beta-carotene, folate; calcium, iron, magnesium, phosphorus, potassium, selenium, zinc

TOFU AND HORSERADISH SAUCE

9 oz. chopped tofu
heaping 2 tbsp. grated
  horseradish
1 tsp. white miso
3 tbsp. unrefined sunflower oil
sea salt, to taste

Put all the ingredients in a food processor with 1 cup water and blend until smooth and creamy. This sauce is particularly delicious served with fish or vegetables.

Mix grated horseradish with vinegar to prevent it from browning and becoming bitter.

butternut squash

NUTRIENTS
Vitamins B1, B3, B5, B6, C, E, K, beta-carotene, folate; calcium, copper, iron, magnesium, phosphorus, potassium, selenium, zinc; fiber; protein; complex carbohydrate

A popular variety of winter squash, this vegetable is a great source of energy-sustaining carbohydrates.

Butternut squash is particularly high in beta-carotene, which is converted into vitamin A in the body and needed for healthy skin and normal immune, digestive, and respiratory tract function. It also contains other carotenoids, including beta-cryptoxanthin, which may significantly lower the risk of lung cancer. Extracts from squash have also been found to reduce the symptoms of benign prostatic hyperplasia, a condition of the prostate gland.

ROASTED BUTTERNUT SQUASH

1 butternut squash
1 tbsp. olive oil
sea salt and ground black pepper

Cut the squash in half lengthwise, remove the seeds, and brush the flesh with the oil. Cook face down in a preheated 425°F oven for 45 minutes until soft. Once cooked, season to taste with the salt and pepper.

agar-agar

This bland, calorie-free seaweed offers a fabulous vegetarian alternative to gelatin for the making of jellos and aspics.

Rich in trace minerals, agar-agar is traditionally used in Japan to help soothe the digestive tract and to relieve constipation. Its high fiber content helps to lower raised cholesterol and suppresses the appetite, making it an ideal food for anyone wanting to lose weight. The main culinary function of this seaweed is as a gelling agent, setting liquids at room temperature. However, it will not set in vinegar or in any foods containing oxalic acid, such as chocolate, rhubarb, and spinach.

NUTRIENTS

Vitamins B2, B3, B5, B6, E, K, folate; calcium, copper, iodine, iron, magnesium, manganese, phosphorus, potassium, selenium, zinc; fiber

REAL FRUIT JELLO

2½ cups chopped soft fruit, (such as peaches, strawberries, grapes)
2½ cups white grape juice
¼ cup agar-agar flakes

Place the chopped fruit in a large heatproof glass bowl and set aside. Put the grape juice and agar-agar in a pan, bring to a boil, and simmer for a few minutes while stirring, until the agar-agar has dissolved. Pour the liquid over the chopped fruit and let cool. Once set, store in the fridge.

031

Ⓒ Ⓥ Ⓞ Ⓞ ⬡ ♡ 〓 🔱 ⚙

kombu

In Japan, this highly nutritious sea vegetable is often used to add flavor to soups, broths and stocks.

Laden with protein and minerals such as calcium, magnesium, potassium, iodine, and iron, kombu improves the nutritional value of any meal into which it is incorporated. It also acts as a tenderizer and is often added to beans to reduce their cooking time and make them easier to digest.

DESTROYS CONTAMINANTS

Heavy metals are common contaminants that can get absorbed into the body where they are stored in organs and tissues. Kombu possesses a fiber molecule called alginic acid which is able to bind to heavy metals such as cadmium, mercury, and lead, and carry them out of the system.

FIGHTS MANY ILLNESSES

A recently discovered substance in kombu called fucoidan has been found to make cancer cells self-destruct. This compound has now been extracted from the seaweed and is available as a nutritional supplement.

Due to kombu's excellent nutrient profile and cleansing abilities, it's claimed to offer relief in a range of health conditions

NUTRIENTS
Vitamins B1, B2, B3, B12, C, beta-carotene; calcium, iodine, iron, magnesium, phosphorus, potassium, sodium; fiber; protein

KOMBU TOMATO BROTH

1 strip dried kombu
6 sun-dried tomatoes

Soak the kombu and tomatoes in 4¼ cups water for 30 minutes, then bring to a boil and simmer for 5 minutes. Remove the kombu and tomatoes. Use the liquid for any recipe that includes broth. The kombu can be reused to make more broth or added to beans or casseroles during cooking to enhance flavor.

from rheumatism, arthritis, and high blood pressure to goiter caused by an underactive thyroid.

Being a rich source of glutamic acid—a natural form of the synthetic flavor-enhancer monosodium glutamate (MSG)—kombu is extremely useful when added to stocks, soups, stews, and broths, where it enhances and brings out the flavors of other ingredients.

CANNELLINI KOMBU BEAN POT

heaping 1 cup dried cannellini beans
1 strip dried kombu
½ leek, trimmed and chopped
½ red bell pepper, seeded and chopped
4 cups spinach, chopped

Soak the beans overnight in plenty of cold water. Next day, drain, place in a pan, and cover with 4¼ cups water. Add the kombu, then bring to a boil and simmer, covered, about 2 hours until the beans are soft. Add the leek, red pepper, and spinach, and cook another 15 minutes. Mix well and serve.

nori

NUTRIENTS
Vitamins B1, B3, B5, B6, C, E, K, beta-carotene, folate; calcium, copper, iron, magnesium, phosphorus, potassium, selenium, zinc; fiber; protein; complex carbohydrate

Just one dried sheet of nori seaweed provides the body with as much vitamin A as three eggs.

Used in sushi-making, this "fishy"-tasting seaweed has been cultivated in Japan for over a thousand years. An excellent source of protein, nori helps with growth and tissue repair, and its calcium and iron content nourishes the bones and blood. Particularly high in beta-carotene, nori may help to promote skin health, boost the immune system and slow down eye disease. It also contains vitamin B12, which is rarely found in the plant world, making it an ideal food for strict vegetarians.

NORI POTATO FRITTERS

2 large potatoes, peeled and
   coarsely grated
1 onion, finely chopped
4 cage-free eggs
5 tbsp. nori flakes
1 tbsp. ground mustard
olive oil for shallow frying

Using your hands, squeeze as much of the juice from the grated potatoes as possible, then put them in a bowl and mix them with the onion, eggs, nori, and mustard. Heat the oil in a frying pan, adding the mixture when the oil is hot. Flatten each fritter with a fork and for a few minutes cook on both sides until golden.

wakame

A green leafy sea vegetable, wakame can be soaked and used in salads in place of lettuce.

Traditionally added to miso soup, wakame is mild in flavor and is one of the most popular vegetables from the ocean. It's an excellent source of potassium and may improve heart health by keeping high blood pressure in check. It's also an outstanding source of calcium needed for bone maintenance, and magnesium for relieving stress and muscle tension. In Japan, wakame is used as a blood purifier and is also valued for its nourishing effect on the hair and skin.

NUTRIENTS
Vitamins B3, B5, C, E, K, beta-carotene, folate; calcium, iodine, iron, magnesium, manganese, phosphorus, potassium, selenium, sodium; fiber; protein; omega-3 essential fatty acids

WAKAME NOODLE BROTH

2 tbsp. sesame oil
1 clove garlic, crushed
2 celery stalks, chopped
4¼ cups vegetable broth
1 tbsp. miso
2 carrots, peeled and chopped
8 strips wakame, chopped
2 oz. dried noodles

Put all the ingredients (except the noodles) in a large pot, and bring to a boil, stirring until the miso has dissolved. Simmer, covered, for 30 minutes. Add the noodles and cook a few minutes more until they are cooked through. Serve immediately.

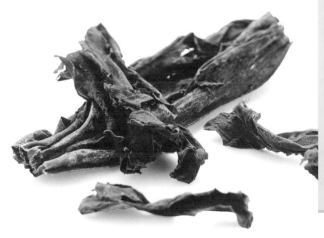

dulse

NUTRIENTS
Vitamins B1, B2, B3, B6, C, beta-carotene; calcium, iodine, iron, magnesium, phosphorus, potassium, sodium, zinc; fiber; protein

This purple-red, peppery seaweed can be added to salads, soups, and casseroles or dry-roasted over an open flame and used as a garnish.

Full of potassium which helps to relieve fluid retention, dulse is also the most iron-rich of the edible seaweeds, making it an excellent food for combating anemia. Like most sea vegetables, it's high in iodine, which is needed to make the thyroid hormone and to help regulate the thyroid gland. A lack of iodine in the diet can result in an underactive thyroid, causing fatigue and weight gain. Eaten in small amounts, dulse is thought to be an effective remedy for sea sickness.

SEA SALAD

3 tbsp. dulse, rinsed
2 handfuls of mixed salad greens
½ cucumber, peeled and chopped
1 scallion, trimmed and chopped
2 tbsp. sesame oil
1 tbsp. rice vinegar
1 tbsp. sesame seeds

Soak the dulse in water for about 3 minutes, then drain and cut it into pieces with scissors. Put it in a large bowl along with the salad greens, cucumber, and scallion. Add the sesame oil and rice vinegar, toss well, and serve sprinkled with sesame seeds.

035

hijiki

This black, wiry sea vegetable has a rich flavor and is delicious added to rice, beans, or stir-fries.

Rich in a broad spectrum of minerals, hijiki is thought to play a contributory role to the thick, shiny hair enjoyed by many Japanese people. It's a superb bone-builder, containing more calcium than any other sea vegetable, and if included in the diet several times a week, it may help to prevent osteoporosis and other bone diseases. Hijiki is also high in fiber, which helps to regulate blood sugar levels and lower elevated cholesterol. Like kombu, it contains the cancer-busting compound, fucoidan.

NUTRIENTS
Vitamins B1, B2, B3, B12, beta-carotene; calcium, iodine, iron, phosphorus, potassium, sodium; fiber; protein

SCRAMBLED EGGS WITH HIJIKI

2 heaping tbsp. hijiki
1 tbsp. olive oil
4 cage-free eggs
6 cherry tomatoes, sliced
2 tbsp. finely chopped chives
1 tsp. ground mustard
1 clove garlic, crushed
sea salt and ground black
    pepper, to taste

Soak the hijiki in water for 15 minutes, then drain and sauté in the oil for about 8 minutes. Meanwhile, beat the eggs in a bowl and add the remaining ingredients. Pour the mixture over the hijiki and cook, stirring frequently until the eggs have thickened but are still soft.

apple

With more varieties now available than ever before, apples are a delicious source of health benefits.

NUTRIENTS
Vitamins B3, C, E, K, beta-carotene, biotin, folate; calcium, chromium, iron, magnesium, manganese, phosphorus, potassium, zinc; fiber; carbohydrate

The old adage "an apple a day keeps the doctor away" could well hold true. According to studies, apples may reduce the risk of several common cancers, as well as protect the brain from the damage that causes conditions such as Alzheimer's and Parkinson's disease. Antioxidant compounds in the skin of apples, in particular quercetin, epicatechin, and procyanidin, are thought to be responsible for this protective action. Apples also contain a soluble fiber called pectin, which lowers high cholesterol levels and regulates digestive function.

APPLE AND APRICOT CRUMBLE

scant 1 cup apple juice
6 apples, peeled, cored, and chopped
10 oz. sugar-free apricot jam
3½ tbsp. unhydrogenated margarine
heaping 1 cup rolled oats
3 tbsp. oat bran

Put the apple juice in a pan and bring to a boil. Add the apples and simmer, covered, until the liquid evaporates. Mash them, add the jam, and spread in a baking dish. Work the margarine into the oats and oat bran to form a crumble. Spoon it over the fruit and bake in a 350°F oven for about 30 minutes.

pear

Besides making an ideal dessert or snack, pears and pear juice can be used to sweeten cakes and cereals instead of sugar.

Pears are often given as a baby's first fruit, as they are the least likely to cause an allergic reaction. This also makes them one of the best fruits for people with multiple food allergies. The insoluble fiber in pears helps to eliminate cholesterol from the body, which is useful for those at risk of heart disease. Pears also regulate digestion and their vitamin C and folate content boost immunity.

NUTRIENTS
Vitamins B3, C, E, K, beta-carotene, biotin, folate; calcium, iodine, iron, magnesium, phosphorus, potassium, zinc; fiber; carbohydrate

PEARS IN CAROB SAUCE

1¼ cups white grape juice
6 pears, peeled, cored, and cut in half lengthwise
10oz. tofu
3 tbsp. brown rice syrup
2 tbsp. hazelnut butter
1 tsp. carob powder
1 tsp. grain coffee substitute
2 tbsp. unrefined sunflower oil

Put two thirds of the grape juice in a pan and bring to ae boil. Add the pears and simmer, covered, for about 8 minutes until the liquid has evaporated. Divide into four dessert bowls. Put the remaining juice and ingredients in a food processor and blend until creamy, then pour over the pears and serve.

banana

NUTRIENTS
Vitamins B2, C, beta-carotene, folic acid; calcium, copper, iodine, iron, magnesium, manganese, phosphorus, potassium, selenium, zinc; fiber; carbohydrate

Creamy, sweet, and satisfying, bananas are a much-loved fruit for everyone from toddlers to seniors.

Concentrated in easily-digestible carbohydrates and low in fat, bananas are valued for their instant and sustained energy boost. One of the best sources of potassium, they offer protection against high blood pressure and fluid retention and are particularly useful after a bout of diarrhea, which can cause potassium loss. Bananas are also high in tryptophan, an amino acid that the body converts into serotonin, a brain chemical known to improve mood and encourage relaxation.

BANANA MILKSHAKE

2 bananas, chopped
2 cups soy milk or milk of your choice
1 tbsp. maple syrup
1 tbsp. natural vanilla extract
1 tsp. ground nutmeg

Put the first four ingredients in a blender and blend until smooth. Serve chilled, sprinkled with the nutmeg.

Do not refrigerate unripe bananas as they will never ripen.

039

grape

Grapes are very effective at eliminating toxins from the body and cleansing the blood and intestines.

In folk medicine, grapes were used to purify the blood, clean the digestive system, and counter liver and kidney disorders. Their high water and fiber content certainly makes them a useful detoxifying agent. Grapes also contain antioxidants that fight cancer and promote cardiovascular function, including resveratrol found specifically in red grapes. This compound, together with pterostilbene and saponins, aids heart health by reducing the risk of blood clots and relaxing blood vessels.

NUTRIENTS
Vitamins B3, B6, C, K, beta-carotene, biotin, folate; calcium, copper, iodine, iron, magnesium, manganese, phosphorus, potassium, selenium, zinc; fiber; carbohydrate

NON-ALCOHOLIC RED GRAPE SANGRIA

1 apple
3 oranges
1 lime
1 lemon
1 tbsp. agave syrup
4¼ cups red grape juice

Slice the apple and one orange and put them in a glass pitcher. Juice the remaining fruit and add to the pitcher along with the agave syrup and grape juice. Serve chilled with ice.

040

cherry

NUTRIENTS
Vitamins B3, B5, C, beta-carotene, biotin, folate; calcium, iron, magnesium, manganese, phosphorus, potassium, selenium; fiber; carbohydrate

---

CHERRY PARFAIT

2 cups cherries, pitted
2⅓ cups plain live yogurt or soy yogurt
1⅓ cups crunchy granola cereal
2 tbsp. shredded coconut, plus extra for serving
1 tbsp. sugar-free cherry jam (optional)

Put all the ingredients in a food processor and blend until creamy. Serve chilled, sprinkled with extra coconut.

Besides helping to ease pain and inflammation, the naturally-occurring melatonin found in this delicious summer fruit may help to restore irregular sleep patterns.

Packed with anthocyanins, antioxidants which give this fruit its red hue, cherries help to shut down certain enzymes that cause inflammation, so can prevent many kinds of pain. In particular they seem to offer relief from gout—a form of arthritis that occurs when uric acid crystals accumulate in joints, leading to pain and inflammation. In studies, cherries have been found to significantly decrease uric acid levels, so limiting the formation of the gout-inducing crystals.

Cherries can also help to ease pain caused by both osteoarthritis and rheumatoid arthritis, as well as fibromyalgia—pain in the fibrous tissues of the body such as the muscles, tendons, and ligaments.

SLEEP ENHANCERS
Other antioxidants in cherries include superoxide dismutase (useful in joint, respiratory, and gastrointestinal health) and melatonin—one of the most potent known free-radical scavengers ever discovered. Low melatonin levels have been

associated with sleep disturbances such as insomnia, so cherries could be a useful source of this compound, possibly aiding sleep. Melatonin is also important for the function of the immune system.

Proanthocyanidins, another antioxidant found in cherries, have anti-inflammatory activity and can strengthen blood vessels and slow down the aging process of the skin.

CHERRY AND RHUBARB COMPOTE

scant 3 cups cherries, pitted
3 rhubarb stalks, chopped
3 tbsp. apple juice
2 tbsp. fruit sugar
plain live yogurt

Put all the ingredients, except the yogurt, in a pan. Bring to the boil and simmer, covered, for about 8 minutes, stirring occasionally. Serve with the yogurt.

Ⓒ Ⓞ ⬕ ♥ ⊕

date

NUTRIENTS
Vitamins B3, B5, B6, C, K, beta-carotene, biotin, folate; calcium, copper, iodine, iron, magnesium, manganese, phosphorus, potassium, selenium, zinc; fiber; carbohydrate

Available fresh or dried, dates are full of natural sweetness, and make a much healthier snack than refined carbohydrate treats.

Naturally sweet and chewy, dates are perfect for satisfying a sweet tooth without resorting to sugar. They are an excellent source of potassium, important for maintaining fluid and electrolyte balance in the body, and are loaded with fiber, which helps regulate bowel function. The tannin content of dates provides them with an astringent effect, which is of particular benefit for intestinal problems such as diarrhea. As a traditional remedy, it is believed that dates can counteract alcohol intoxication.

STUFFED DATES

1¾ cups ground almonds
¼ cup brown rice syrup
1 tbsp. natural almond extract
12 fresh pitted dates
12 almonds (or nuts of your choice)

Combine the ground almonds, brown rice syrup, and almond extract together until a paste is formed. Cut the dates almost in half lengthwise, being careful not to cut all the way through, and stuff each one with almond paste. Top each date with an almond for serving.

fig

Front-runners in the calcium stakes, figs can help to boost levels of this key bone-building mineral.

Although it's not apparent, figs are one of the best sources of calcium, vital for bone growth in children and bone density in adults. They also contain more fiber than any other dried or fresh fruit, aiding satiety by promoting a feeling of fullness in the stomach and helping to balance blood sugar levels. In addition, their high fiber content provides a laxative effect, which is of benefit to those who suffer from chronic constipation.

NUTRIENTS
Vitamins B3, B5, B6, C, beta-carotene, biotin, folate; calcium, copper, iodine, iron, magnesium, manganese, phosphorus, potassium, zinc; fiber; carbohydrate

HONEY-BAKED FIGS

8 fresh figs
¼ cup clear honey
¼ cup chopped nuts
½ cup plain live Greek yogurt

Trim the end of the stalks off the figs, then cut a cross in the top of each one to open them out. Mix together the honey and nuts, and spoon the mixture into the top of the figs. Place them in a baking dish and cook in a preheated 375°F oven for about 15 minutes until the figs are soft. Serve with the yogurt.

Ⓒ Ⓞ Ⓔ Ⓔ Ⓞ ⊕ ⊛

prune

With one of the highest antioxidant rankings of all fruit, there's much more to prunes than their ability to prevent constipation.

Prunes are dried plums, both of which have made headlines in relation to their rich phytochemical content, namely neochlorogenic and chlorogenic acids. These antioxidant compounds help to neutralize hazardous free radicals in the body, helping to protect cells from damage and slow down the aging process. Eating prunes is also a sweet way of increasing beta-carotene, potassium, iron, and fiber intake. In addition, prunes contain a natural laxative called diphenylisatin, which is why they are so useful for keeping the bowel regular.

NUTRIENTS
Vitamins B2, B3, B5, B6, beta-carotene, folate; calcium, copper, iodine, iron, magnesium, manganese, phosphorus, potassium, selenium, zinc; fiber; carbohydrate

AROMATIC STEWED PRUNES

1⅔ cups soft pitted prunes
juice of 2 oranges
pinch of ground cinnamon

Put the prunes in a pan with the orange juice and cinnamon, bring to a boil, then simmer, covered, for about 15 minutes. Serve with yogurt for breakfast or on their own as a dessert.

blueberry

Blueberries are the number one fruit for helping to protect cells from free radical damage and aging.

According to research, blueberries rank top in antioxidant activity compared to 40 other fresh fruit and vegetables. They get their beautiful blue color from anthocyanins, potent antioxidants that help to neutralize cancer-forming substances in the body. Their other phytochemicals include proanthocyanidins, which protect the eyes, skin, and blood vessels, and pterostilbene, which has antidiabetic and cholesterol-lowering properties and may reduce cognitive decline. Blueberries are a fine source of vitamin C and they also contain antibacterial agents.

NUTRIENTS
Vitamins B3, B5, C, K, beta-carotene, folate; calcium, iron, magnesium, manganese, phosphorus, potassium, selenium, zinc; fiber; carbohydrate

BLUEBERRY FOOL

1 lb., 2 oz. tofu
scant 1 cup apple juice
2 cups blueberries, plus extra
    for serving
1¼ cups agave syrup
⅓ cup unrefined sunflower oil
1 tsp. natural vanilla extract

Put the tofu and apple juice in a food processor and blend until smooth. Add the remaining ingredients and continue to blend until thick and creamy. Spoon into dessert glasses and serve chilled, decorated with a few blueberries on top.

cranberry

NUTRIENTS
Vitamins B5, C, K, beta-carotene, folate; calcium, iron, magnesium, phosphorus, potassium, selenium; fiber; carbohydrate

---

CRANBERRY AND BANANA SMOOTHIE

1¼ cups unsweetened cranberry juice
1¼ cups white grape juice
2 bananas, chopped
10 strawberries, hulled
1¾ cups plain live yogurt or soy yogurt
3 tbsp. honey

Put all the ingredients in a blender and whiz until smooth. Drink immediately.

Research has now confirmed the commonly believed folk wisdom that cranberries can prevent and treat urinary tract infections.

A popular remedy for treating cystitis, cranberries contain components that interfere with the adherence of bacteria to the lining of the urinary tract, allowing them to be flushed out more easily. Other compounds in this berry have been found to inhibit plaque-causing bacteria in the mouth, which causes tooth decay and gum disease. Cranberries also promote powerful anticancer activity and can combat kidney stone formation.

Look for cranberry juices that are sweetened with apple juice rather than sugar.

046

raspberry

Delicious and extremely nutritious, raspberries make a handy, health-giving alternative to sweets.

Bursting with antioxidants, the regular consumption of raspberries protects against many conditions, including inflammatory diseases, allergies, cardiovascular disease, age-related cognitive decline, and cancer. They are particularly high in ellagic acid, which is thought to lower high cholesterol, reduce the risk of heart disease, and promote the healing of wounds. On top of this, raspberries possess antibacterial properties, are an excellent source of vitamin C, and are a rich source of fiber.

NUTRIENTS

Vitamins B3, B5, C, E, K, beta-carotene, biotin, folate; calcium, copper, iodine, iron, magnesium, manganese, phosphorus, potassium, selenium, zinc; fiber; carbohydrate

RASPBERRY COULIS

1 lb. raspberries
1 tbsp. fruit sugar
1 tsp. lemon juice

Put all the ingredients in a food processor and blend. Pour the mixture through a fine strainer into a bowl, pressing on the solids. Serve the sauce on top of ice cream or other desserts.

goji berry

NUTRIENTS
Vitamins B1, B2, B6, C, E, beta-carotene, folate; calcium, iron, phosphorus, potassium, selenium, zinc; fiber; protein; carbohydrate; omega-3 and omega-6 essential fatty acids

LUXURY TRAIL MIX

Mix together 2 handfuls of goji berries with a handful of each of the following: sunflower seeds, pumpkin seeds, almonds, pine nuts, raisins, chopped dried dates, chopped dried banana, and coconut shreds—plus any other favorite dried fruit or nuts. This makes a tasty, power-packed snack.

In China, it is said that eating a handful of goji berries each morning will lift your mood and make you feel happy for the entire day.

Only available in their dried state outside of their production regions of China, Tibet, and Mongolia, these vibrant orange-red berries are claimed to be one of the world's most powerful anti-aging foods. Besides containing a remarkable range of essential nutrients, they possess several phytochemicals, including zeaxanthin, which protects against eye disease, solavetivone, an antibacterial agent, and physalin, an antileukaemia compound. The berries also supply special polysaccharides, which have antioxidant properties and can enhance immunity.

açai berry

With their spectacular nutritional and antioxidant profile, these berries may be one of the healthiest foods on the planet.

NUTRIENTS
Vitamins B1, B2, B3, C, E, beta-carotene; calcium, copper, magnesium, phosphorus, potassium, zinc; fiber; protein; carbohydrate; monounsaturated fats, omega-3 and omega-6 essential fatty acids

Native to the Amazon rainforest, açai berries (pronounced "a-sigh-ee") deteriorate quickly after harvesting, so are normally available only as a juice or fruit pulp to nonlocals. They have recently created a stir because of their incredible nutritional content, which includes protein, monounsaturated fats, omega-6 and omega-3 essential fatty acids, and many vitamins and minerals. Even more impressive is the fruit's phytochemical content with beta-sitosterol that reduces cholesterol, and numerous antioxidants, such as anthocyanins which have anticancer and anti-inflammatory properties, and proanthocyanidins which strengthen blood vessels.

AÇAI-BLUEBERRY WHIZ

1¼ cups açai juice
2½ cups apple juice
1½ cups blueberries
6 strawberries, hulled

Put all the ingredients in a blender and whiz until smooth. Drink immediately.

tangerine

NUTRIENTS
Vitamins B3, B5, C, E, K,
beta-carotene, biotin, folate;
calcium, iodine, iron, magnesium,
phosphorus, potassium, selenium,
zinc; fiber; carbohydrate

Ward off winter colds and flu with this juicy citrus fruit, which is high in immunity-boosting vitamin C.

This sweet and tangy citrus fruit is a cross between a mandarin and a bitter orange. It's an excellent source of both vitamin C and beta-carotene, important nutrients for skin maintenance and immune function, and also contains folic acid, which is needed to make red blood cells. Additionally, tangerines are endowed with three phytochemicals: hesperidin, a flavonoid that protects the heart, and tangeritin and limonene, which have been found to guard against various forms of cancer.

EXOTIC FRUIT MEDLEY

2 tangerines, peeled and
   segmented
2 mangoes, peeled, pitted,
   and chopped
2 kiwi fruit, peeled and
   chopped
1 papaya, peeled and chopped
¼ pineapple, peeled and
   chopped
a handful of blueberries
juice of 1 lime
1 tbsp. agave syrup

Put all the fruit in a large bowl.
Add the lime juice and agave
syrup and mix. Serve with
yogurt, crème fraîche, or a
dairy-free alternative.

050

grapefruit

This sharp-tasting citrus fruit may help healthy weight reduction by boosting the metabolism.

Grapefruits come in many shades, from white to red. The pink and red ones are colored by lycopene, a carotenoid with anticancer activity. Consumed first thing in the morning, grapefruit can prevent constipation, while eaten before a meal it can stimulate the taste buds. Its low calorie count and glycemic index make it good for weight loss, along with its metabolism-stimulating action, which helps to burn fat. Grapefruit also contains vitamin C, as well as pectin to lower cholesterol, and bioflavonoids to strengthen blood capillaries.

NUTRIENTS
Vitamins B3, B5, C, E, beta-carotene, biotin, folate; calcium, iodine, iron, magnesium, phosphorus, potassium; fiber; carbohydrate

CITRUS FRUIT SALAD

3 large handfuls of mixed salad greens
2 tbsp. chopped parsley
1 tbsp. chopped cilantro
1 tbsp. sunflower seeds
½ pink grapefruit
1 tbsp. olive oil
1 tbsp. lemon juice
1 tbsp. orange juice

Put the salad greens, parsley, cilantro, and sunflower seeds in a large bowl. Cut the grapefruit into segments and add them to the bowl. Drizzle the olive oil and citrus juices over the salad, then gently toss and serve immediately.

lemon

NUTRIENTS

Vitamins B3, B5, B6, C, E, beta-carotene, biotin, folate; calcium, copper, iodine, iron, magnesium, manganese, phosphorus, potassium, selenium, zinc; fiber; carbohydrate

Hot water with lemon juice and honey is one of the best natural remedies for soothing a sore throat.

Although lemons are not snack material, their health benefits can be reaped by using their freshly squeezed juice in salad dressings or as a flavoring agent in drinks and baked goods. Their high vitamin C content, along with natural antiseptic properties, makes them an effective remedy for sore throats, colds, flu, and other infections. Lemons also stimulate the gallbladder, which in turn aids liver and digestive function. A compound called limonene, which also has anticancer activity, is responsible for this effect.

SUGAR-FREE LEMONADE

3¼ cups club soda
2⅔ cups white grape juice
juice of 3 lemons
1 tbsp. agave syrup

Put all the ingredients in a glass pitcher and stir. Serve chilled with plenty of ice.

guava

With their rich aroma and vibrant creamy flesh, guavas are delectable in homemade smoothies.

The flavor of this small tropical fruit has been described as a cross between strawberry, pear, and pineapple. Containing more vitamin C than citrus fruit, guavas help bolster the immune system, while their excellent beta-carotene content promotes healthy eyes and skin. They are also a good source of calcium, which is needed by the skeletal system, and are traditionally used to treat diarrhea. According to studies, guavas have blood sugar-lowering properties that may be of benefit to people with diabetes.

NUTRIENTS
Vitamins B3, B5, B6, C, E, beta-carotene, biotin, folate; calcium, copper, iodine, iron, magnesium, manganese, phosphorus, potassium, selenium, zinc; fiber; carbohydrate

MANGO-GUAVA LASSI

1 mango, peeled, pitted, and chopped
1 guava, chopped
1¾ cups apple juice
1 cup milk or soy milk
¾ cup rice milk
1 tsp. ground cardamom, plus extra for sprinkling

Put all the ingredients in a blender and blend until smooth. Sprinkle with a pinch of ground cardamom and drink immediately.

053

🌀 C 🖐 🅞 🍃 ❤ ✳

pomegranate

NUTRIENTS
Vitamins B3, B5, B6, C, E,
beta-carotene, biotin, folate;
calcium, copper, iron, magnesium,
phosphorus, potassium, selenium,
zinc; fiber; carbohydrate

To remove
seeds from a
pomegranate, tap it
on the skin side with
a wooden spoon
until they fall out.

Steeped in symbolism since ancient times, pomegranate now has superfood status, thanks to recent research into its healing attributes.

The edible seed clusters can make eating this fruit tricky, although with so many health rewards on offer, it's well worth the effort. Pomegranate is abundant in antioxidants called punicalagins, which have been shown to prevent several forms of cancer by protecting the body against free radicals, which can damage

FRUIT SALAD WITH POMEGRANATE

1 pomegranate
medium bunch white seedless
    grapes, destalked
1½ cups strawberries, hulled
    and chopped
1 banana, chopped
1 peach, pitted and chopped
¾ cup blueberries
¼ cup fruit juice of choice
1 tbsp. lemon juice
1 tbsp. honey
pinch of ground nutmeg

Scoop out the seeds from the pomegranate and put them in a bowl along with the other fruit. Combine the fruit juice, lemon juice, and honey, pour it over the fruit, and mix gently. Serve sprinkled with the nutmeg.

cells. In fact, according to studies, one glass of pomegranate juice contains almost three times as many antioxidants as the same amount of red wine, green tea, or orange juice.

A HEALTHY HEART

In relation to heart disease, pomegranate not only lowers high blood pressure but helps to fight LDL (bad) cholesterol, which is linked to heart attacks and strokes. Furthermore, it appears to slow down cartilage deterioration in osteoarthritis, a condition in which the joints are gradually worn down over time by wear and tear. On the nutrient front, this fruit provides vitamin C and potassium, both of which add to its heart health benefits.

Pomegranate is also thought to have antiviral and antibacterial properties, and has been shown to discourage the formation of dental plaque.

POMEGRANATE AND PEACH NECTAR

2½ cups pomegranate juice
2 peaches, pitted and chopped

Put the ingredients in a blender and whiz until smooth. Drink immediately.

⊙◐◎◆◑♡≡❋

kiwi fruit

NUTRIENTS
Vitamins B3, B5, B6, C, E, beta-carotene, biotin, folate; calcium, copper, iodine, iron, magnesium, manganese, phosphorus, potassium, selenium, zinc; fiber; carbohydrate

---

GRILLED FRUIT KEBABS

3 kiwi fruit, peeled
½ pineapple, peeled
3 bananas
16 strawberries
scant ½ cup pineapple juice
2 tbsp. agave syrup or honey

Cut the kiwis, pineapple, and bananas into 1-in. cubes. Thread alternate pieces of the cut-up fruit and strawberries onto wooden skewers. Combine the pineapple juice and agave syrup or honey in a bowl and use it to brush the kebabs. Then, place them under a broiler for about 6 minutes, turning frequently.

Named after an indigenous New Zealand bird, kiwi fruit can combat the factors that cause heart disease and stroke.

Kiwi fruit have been found to have an anticlotting effect, which is good news for people who are at high risk of heart disease and strokes. According to research, blood clotting was significantly reduced in those consuming two to three kiwi fruit a day. With further studies, this fruit could possibly become a natural alternative to aspirin as a blood-thinning agent. In addition, kiwis act as a mild laxative, probably owing to their fiber content, and are a rich source of cell-protective antioxidants including vitamins C and E, beta-carotene, and the phytochemical lutein, which helps to boost eye health.

papaya

Also known as paw paw, papaya can be eaten ripe as a succulent fresh fruit or cooked in curries and stews in its unripe green state.

Besides being a superb source of vitamin C and beta-carotene, which are important for the skin and immune system, papaya contains an enzyme called papain, which promotes the digestion of protein. Papain also soothes inflammation, so may be beneficial in easing joint pain from conditions such as arthritis and sports injuries. Used topically, papaya flesh is said to aid the healing of skin sores, while its edible seeds have been used to treat stomach aches and fungal infections.

NUTRIENTS
Vitamins B3, B5, C, beta-carotene, biotin, folate; calcium, iodine, iron, magnesium, manganese, phosphorus, potassium, selenium, zinc; fiber; carbohydrate

GET-UP-AND-GO JUICE

1¾ cups apple juice
½ papaya, peeled and sliced
2 apricots, pitted and chopped
¼ avocado, peeled, pitted, and chopped
heaping 1 cup plain live yogurt
pinch of ground nutmeg

Put all the ingredients (except the nutmeg) in a blender and whiz until smooth. Serve sprinkled with nutmeg.

pineapple

Not only a delicious exotic fruit, pineapple has a special health asset in the form of bromelain, an enzyme that helps in the digestion of protein.

Research has shown that bromelain also works as an anti-inflammatory and is useful for the treatment of sprains, muscle injuries, and post-operative inflammation by reducing pain and swelling. Pineapple is also a good source of manganese, an essential trace mineral needed for skin, bone, and cartilage formation, and vitamin C, which mops up dangerous free radicals and enhances immune function.

POACHED PINEAPPLE

scant 1 cup grape juice
1 tbsp. honey
½ pineapple, thickly sliced
juice of ½ orange

Put the grape juice and honey in a pan and bring to a boil. Add the pineapple and poach for 5 minutes. Place in a baking dish, squeeze the orange juice over it and cook in a preheated 400°F oven for 10 minutes. Remove, return juices to the pan and heat until reduced to a syrup. Pour it over the pineapple and serve.

persimmon

This tasty bright orange fruit can be eaten like an apple or pear, with or without the skin.

NUTRIENTS
Vitamin C, beta-carotene, folate; calcium, iron, magnesium, phosphorus, potassium; fiber; carbohydrate

Persimmon, also known as Sharon fruit, was called "the food of the gods" by the ancient Greeks. It contains a broad range of nutrients including vitamin C, potassium, magnesium, calcium, and fiber, all of which are vital for maintaining a healthy heart and keeping cholesterol levels in check. The fruit is also a good source of beta-carotene, which is required for the health of the skin and mucus membranes, and for night vision. Persimmon juice is believed to combat hangovers by lowering the density of alcohol in the blood.

RAINBOW FRUIT SALAD WITH CHOPPED NUTS AND RAISINS

4 persimmons
8 lychees, peeled and pitted
1 banana
8 fresh pitted dates
a handful of chopped hazelnuts
a handful of raisins
juice of 1 orange (or other fruit juice, if you prefer)

Chop the persimmons, lychees, banana, and dates, and put them in a bowl along with the nuts and raisins. Pour the orange juice over the fruit, stir gently, and serve.

oats

For blood sugar maintenance, sustained energy, and staving off hunger, there's no better breakfast than a steaming bowl of cooked oatmeal.

The main feature in oats is a soluble fiber compound called beta-glucan, which decreases the glucose and insulin response after eating. This action makes it a beneficial food for diabetics or those with blood-sugar imbalances. Oats also enhance the immune system and significantly lower LDL (bad) cholesterol levels. In addition, they contain unique antioxidant compounds called avenanthramides, which prevent free-radical damage, thereby offering protection against cancer and heart disease.

RAISIN OAT BARS

3 cups rolled oats
¾ cup raisins
⅔ cup unhydrogenated
   margarine
½ cup honey
6 tbsp. fruit sugar
1 tbsp. natural vanilla extract

Put the oats and raisins in a mixing bowl and set aside. Melt the margarine in a pan, add the remaining ingredients, and stir. Pour onto the oats and mix well. Press into a nonstick baking tray, and cook in a preheated 375ºF oven 15 to18 minutes.

barley

This glutinous grain has a chewy texture similar to pasta and is ideal eaten in soups and stews during the winter months to help warm the body.

An excellent source of slow-releasing carbohydrates, barley helps stabilize blood sugar levels, thereby preventing energy slumps and sugar cravings. It's also high in B-vitamins, which help to boost energy and combat stress, and a soluble fiber compound called beta-glucan that lowers raised cholesterol levels. Barley water, a drink made from the liquid in which barley has been boiled, is traditionally acclaimed for treating diarrhea, fluid retention, and cystitis.

Choose "pot" barley rather than "pearl" barley, as it is less refined and therefore has more nutrients.

NUTRIENTS
Vitamins B1, B2, B3, B5, B6, E, K, beta-carotene, folate; calcium, copper, iron, magnesium, manganese, phosphorus, potassium, silica, zinc; fiber; protein; complex carbohydrate

BARLEY AND VEGETABLE SOUP

¼ cup pot barley, hulled and soaked overnight in cold water
2 tbsp. olive oil
1 onion, chopped
1 clove garlic, crushed
2 celery stalks, chopped
1 tomato, chopped
1 tbsp. paprika
2 oz. green beans, chopped
6½ cups vegetable broth
1 tsp. dried mixed herbs

Drain the barley and put it in a large pan. Add all the other ingredients, then bring to a boil and simmer, covered, for about 1 hour.

brown rice

NUTRIENTS
Vitamins B1, B3, B5, B6, E, K, biotin, folate; calcium, copper, iodine, iron, magnesium, manganese, phosphorus, potassium, selenium, zinc; fiber; protein; complex carbohydrate

Providing more than one fifth of the calories eaten worldwide, rice, particularly in its unrefined form, is one of the most nourishing food sources available.

According to the macrobiotic philosophy, brown rice is considered to be the most balanced of all foods and those who follow this dietary regime often eat it on a daily basis. When consumed regularly it may help to ease depression, probably due to its B-vitamin and magnesium content—nutrients needed to calm and strengthen the nerves. It also helps stabilize blood sugar levels and makes a wonderful convalescing food.

PILAF RICE

1 onion, finely chopped
1 tbsp. olive oil
2 cardamom pods
5 cloves
½ cinnamon stick
pinch of saffron threads
1 cup brown basmati rice
3⅓ cups vegetable broth
2 bay leaves

Sauté the onion in the oil until soft. Add the spices and cook for another 2 minutes. Then add the rice and stir until the grains are coated in the oil before adding the broth and bay leaves. Bring to a boil, then simmer, covered, for about 50 minutes or until the rice is soft and all the liquid has been absorbed.

TOXIN FIGHTER

Brown rice is a good source of insoluble fiber, helping to normalize and regulate bowel function, prevent constipation, and remove toxins from the large intestine. Gamma oryzanol, a compound present in rice bran, may help to lower elevated cholesterol by increasing its excretion and reducing the absorption of cholesterol from food. Gamma oryzanol has also been found to aid in the relief of gastritis and other gastrointestinal complaints.

GO FOR BROWN

The processing of wholegrain brown rice into white rice removes much of its B-vitamin and mineral content and all of its dietary fiber. So although brown rice takes a little longer to cook than white rice—about 45 minutes as opposed to 15 minutes—it's well worth the extra time.

COCONUT MILK RICE PUDDING

1 cup short-grain brown rice
3 tbsp. raisins
2 tbsp. agave syrup
1 cinnamon stick
10 cardamom pods
1¾ cups coconut milk
½ tsp. natural vanilla extract
ground cinnamon

Put the rice, raisins, agave syrup, cinnamon stick, and cardamom with 4¼ cups water in a pan and bring to a boil. Simmer, covered, for 90 minutes until the water has been absorbed. Add the coconut milk and vanilla extract, and cook for 5 minutes. Serve hot or cold, sprinkled with the ground cinnamon.

millet

NUTRIENTS
Vitamins B1, B2, B3, B5, B6, E, K, folate; calcium, copper, iron, magnesium, manganese, phosphorus, potassium, selenium, silica, zinc; fiber; protein; complex carbohydrate

This small, round grain helps to feed the skin, hair, and nails, and being free of gluten, it is well tolerated by most people.

Unlike most grains, millet is alkaline-forming, so it may help to neutralize acidic conditions in the body, such as rheumatism and arthritis. It's an excellent source of minerals, particularly calcium, magnesium, and silica, all needed for healthy skin and strong hair and nails. In addition, magnesium plays an important role in hormonal balance, easing menstrual discomfort and water retention. As millet does not contain the gluten that wheat, barley, and oats have, it is suitable for those with coeliac disease or other forms of gluten intolerance.

MILLET PATTIES

1¼ millet
1 tbsp. olive oil
1 tbsp. tomato paste
2 tbsp. vegetable stock
1 tbsp. tamari
2 tbsp. unrefined sunflower oil

Bring 3¼ cups water to a boil in a pan, add the millet, and simmer, covered, for 45 minutes. Add the remaining ingredients (except the oil) and mix well. Form into patties, brush with oil, and cook in a 375ºF preheated oven for 40 minutes, turning them over halfway through.

quinoa

For centuries this grain-like seed sustained the Incas of South America and today it has superfood status thanks to its exceptional nutritional profile.

Unlike traditional cereals such as wheat and rice, quinoa contains all eight essential amino acids, making it a complete source of protein, normally found only in meat, fish, eggs, dairy, and soy. This means that it's an ideal food for strict vegetarians or anyone who wants to boost their protein intake, such as athletes and those on high-protein weight-loss diets. Quinoa is also an excellent source of calcium and magnesium, which are needed for the bones, and iron, which prevents anemia.

NUTRIENTS
Vitamins B1, B2, B3, B5, B6, E, folate; calcium, copper, iron, magnesium, manganese, phosphorus, potassium, zinc; fiber; protein; complex carbohydrate

QUINOA TABBOULEH

scant 2¼ cups vegetable broth
1½ cups quinoa
3 tomatoes, chopped
½ cucumber, peeled and
**   chopped**
4 scallions, trimmed and
**   chopped**
heaping ⅓ cup chopped
**   parsley**
2 cloves garlic, crushed
2 tbsp. olive oil
2 tbsp. lemon juice
sea salt and ground black
**   pepper, to taste**

Bring the broth to a boil in a pan and simmer the quinoa, covered, for 15 minutes. Transfer to a bowl, add the remaining ingredients, and mix.

⊙⦿⊜♡⊜⊕⊛

amaranth

NUTRIENTS
Vitamins B1, B2, B3, B5, B6,
C, E, folate; calcium, copper,
iron, magnesium, phosphorus,
potassium, zinc; fiber; protein;
complex carbohydrate

A staple for the Aztec civilization of central Mexico, this tiny, nutritious grain is super-rich in protein, calcium, and iron.

Like quinoa, amaranth is a fantastic source of complete protein, along with fiber and complex carbohydrates. It is also high in calcium and contains more iron than most grains, so when eaten regularly can boost levels of this mineral. Several studies have shown that amaranth can reduce blood pressure and high cholesterol, as well as enhance the immune system. The active components responsible for these effects are thought to be plant stanols and squalene, important phytochemicals.

AMARANTH PANCAKES

½ cup amaranth
1 tbsp. arrowroot powder
1 tsp. baking powder
pinch of sea salt
1 cage-free egg
scant 1 cup soy milk
1 tbsp. honey
2 tbsp. unrefined sunflower oil

Grind the amaranth into a flour and put it in a bowl with the arrowroot powder, baking powder, and salt. Add the egg, soy milk, and honey, and mix well. Pour a quarter of the batter into an oiled frying pan and cook on each side for 2 minutes. Repeat until all the batter is used up.

⊙ ◉ ◐ ⬘ ♡ ⬤ ⊕

buckwheat

This unique-tasting grain blends well when mixed with blander grains and is marvelous for strengthening blood vessels and improving a sluggish circulation.

In spite of its name, buckwheat is not related to wheat and is suitable for those on a wheat- or gluten-free diet. Its main asset is its rich source of rutin, a bioflavonoid compound that helps strengthen weakened blood capillaries. In turn, this may improve circulatory problems such as capillary fragility, chilblains, and high blood pressure. Buckwheat also appears to address glucose intolerance by aiding blood-sugar balance.

NUTRIENTS
Vitamins B1, B2, B3, B5, B6, E, K, folate; calcium, copper, iron, magnesium, manganese, phosphorus, potassium, selenium, zinc; fiber; protein; complex carbohydrate

Soba are a type of thin Japanese noodle, often made from buckwheat flour.

SOBA NOODLES IN PESTO SAUCE

¼ cup olive oil
2 onions, chopped
2 cloves garlic, crushed
8 tomatoes, chopped
heaping ⅓ cup chopped basil
2 tsp. dried basil
heaping ⅓ cup pine nuts
1 lb., 2 oz. soba (buckwheat) noodles

Heat the oil in a pan and sauté the onion. Add the garlic and tomatoes and simmer, covered, for 20 minutes. Stir in the basil and pine nuts and cook for a few minutes. Put the mixture in a food processor and blend until creamy. Meanwhile, boil the soba noodles in water until *al dente* and serve with the pesto sauce.

aduki bean

NUTRIENTS
Vitamins B1, B3, B5, B6, E, beta-carotene, biotin, folate; calcium, copper, iodine, iron, magnesium, manganese, phosphorus, potassium, selenium, zinc; fiber; protein; complex carbohydrate

Try sprouting aduki beans since they are one of the easiest legumes to grow.

In Japan, these small, red legumes are known as the "king of beans" and are the second most popular legume after the soy bean.

Containing more fiber and protein and less fat than most beans, adukis are the legumes of choice for anyone wanting to lose weight. Their high potassium content, which acts as a natural diuretic, adds to this weight-reducing effect by ridding the body of excess fluid. A drink made from the water in which aduki beans have been boiled is a traditional remedy for kidney and bladder complaints.

ADUKI BEAN CHILI

½ cup aduki beans
1 onion, chopped
1 clove garlic, crushed
2 tbsp. olive oil
14 oz. can chopped tomatoes
½ green chili, seeded and finely chopped
½ tsp. chili powder
1 tbsp. tamari

Soak the beans overnight in cold water. Next day, drain, put in a pan with water and bring to a boil. Simmer, covered, for about 1 hour until soft. Drain and set aside. In another pan, gently fry the onion and garlic in the oil, add the remaining ingredients and the beans, and simmer, covered, for 25 minutes.

chickpea

Eaten as part of a balanced diet, chickpeas can help to keep high cholesterol in check and protect against heart disease.

High in both insoluble and soluble fiber, chickpeas not only maintain a healthy digestive system but significantly reduce both total and LDL (bad) cholesterol. Their role in heart health is also associated with their folate content, which lowers a compound called homocysteine in the blood, an excess of which is a risk factor for heart attack and stroke. Being rich in complex carbohydrates, chickpeas provide sustaining energy, while their substantial iron content may help to stave off anemia.

NUTRIENTS
Vitamins B1, B2, B3, B5, B6, E, K, beta-carotene, biotin, folate; calcium, copper, iodine, iron, magnesium, manganese, phosphorus, potassium, selenium, zinc; fiber; protein; complex carbohydrate

CHICKPEA CURRY

5½ oz. chickpeas
1 onion, chopped
2 cloves garlic, crushed
2 tsp. curry powder
2 tbsp. olive oil
2 cups tomato puree

Soak the chickpeas overnight in cold water. Next day, drain and put in a pan with water. Bring to a boil and simmer, covered, for 2 hours until soft. Drain and set aside. Then, sauté the onion, garlic, and curry powder in the oil, stirring continually. Add the tomto puree and cooked chickpeas and simmer, covered, for 25 minutes.

lentil

NUTRIENTS

Vitamins B1, B2, B3, B5, B6, E, K, beta-carotene, biotin, folate; calcium, copper, iodine, iron, magnesium, manganese, phosphorus, potassium, selenium, zinc; fiber; protein; complex carbohydrate

Lentils come in several varieties, including green, brown, red split and French, and are one of the best foods for balancing blood sugar levels.

With their low glyemic index and complex carbohydrate content, lentils can prevent energy slumps by sustaining blood- sugar balance. They are also an excellent source of insoluble fiber, which helps to keep the bowel regular, as well as soluble fiber, which lowers high cholesterol levels. In addition to providing slow-releasing body fuel, lentils may help to combat fatigue by replenishing iron and B-vitamin stores.

RED LENTIL DAL

2 tbsp. olive oil
1 onion, chopped
2 cloves garlic, crushed
1 tsp. ground mustard
1 tsp. ground cumin
½ tsp. chili powder
½ tsp. turmeric
2 tomatoes, chopped
1 cup red lentils

Heat the oil in a pan and gently fry the onion until soft. Add the garlic, spices, and tomatoes, and simmer for a few minutes, stirring. Add the lentils and scant 2¼ cups water, bring to a boil, and simmer, covered, for 20 minutes.

Lentils are best eaten with whole grains where they fulfill the requirement of a complete protein.

soy bean

The health benefits of soy can be enjoyed in its many forms, such as tofu, tempe, edamame, soy milk, miso, shoyu, and tamari.

Unlike other legumes, soy is a source of complete protein, rivaling meat, fish, and eggs. It is also rich in brain-boosting nutrients including essential fatty acids and lecithin, and contains isoflavones, a type of plant estrogen, found to help balance estrogen levels in the body. This makes soy useful in circumstances where estrogen levels may be out of kilter, such as during menopause. Soy isoflavones also appear to increase bone mass, offering protection against osteoporosis.

NUTRIENTS
Vitamins B1, B2, B3, B5, B6, E, K, beta-carotene, biotin, folate; calcium, copper, iodine, iron, magnesium, manganese, phosphorus, potassium, selenium, zinc; fiber; protein; complex carbohydrate; omega-3 and omega-6 essential fatty acids; lecithin

TOFU SCRAMBLER

1 lb., 2 oz. tofu
2 tsp. dried mixed herbs
2 tsp. paprika
2 tsp. ground mustard
2 tsp. tamari
2 tbsp. chopped, flat-leaf parsley
3 tbsp. olive oil
¼ cup vegetable broth
1 onion, chopped

Mash the tofu in a bowl and mix in the dried herbs, paprika, mustard, tamari, and parsley. Set aside. Heat the oil and vegetable broth in a pan and gently fry the onion until soft. Add the tofu mixture and cook for about 8 minutes, stirring frequently.

almond

Crammed with goodness, these creamy-tasting nuts are ideal food for the brain and nervous system.

NUTRIENTS
Vitamins B1, B2, B3, B5, B6, E, biotin, folate; calcium, copper, iodine, iron, magnesium, manganese, phosphorus, potassium, selenium, zinc; fiber; protein; monounsaturated fats, omega-6 essential fatty acids

One of the most health-giving of all nuts, almonds are packed with nutrition. Their calcium and magnesium content aids bone-building and muscle function, while their high levels of vitamin E improve the skin, protect cells from free radicals, and slow down the aging process. Almonds also contain monounsaturated fats, which lower cholesterol levels. They are a rich source of protein, making them great for vegetarians. While high fat foods often cause weight gain, an almond-enriched diet has been found to help shed unwanted pounds.

RASPBERRY ALMOND TART

1 cup sugar-free raspberry jam
1 cage-free egg, beaten
5 tbsp. brown rice syrup
1 cup ground almonds
¼ cup unrefined sunflower oil
5 tbsp. rice milk
½ tsp. natural vanilla extract
4 drops natural almond extract

Spread the jam into the bottom of a baking dish. Put the remaining ingredients in a bowl, mix well, and spoon the mixture evenly over the jam. Bake in a preheated 375°F oven 40 to 45 minutes until golden and firm to the touch.

070

macadamia nut

High in monounsaturated fats, macadamias help to normalize blood cholesterol levels and improve overall heart health.

NUTRIENTS
Vitamins B1, B3, B5, B6, E, biotin; calcium, copper, iodine, iron, magnesium, manganese, phosphorus, potassium, selenium, zinc; fiber; protein; monounsaturated fats

Including macadamias regularly in the diet reduces LDL (bad) cholesterol levels, while increasing good HDL cholesterol. This effect is linked to the nut's high concentration of monounsaturated fats along with its plant sterol content, which inhibits the absorption of cholesterol from food. Macadamias are full of other nutrients, including potassium and magnesium, which help to regulate fluid balance, protein needed for growth and tissue repair, and cell-protective antioxidants such as vitamin E, selenium, and a compound called epicatechin.

MACADAMIA CRANBERRY CRUNCH

¾ cup macadamia nuts
¾ cup dried cranberries
2⅓ cups rolled oats
2 tbsp. brown rice syrup
2 tbsp. unrefined sunflower oil
1 tbsp. natural vanilla extract

Crush the nuts into small pieces in a food processor, then mix them with the other ingredients. Spread the mixture on a baking tray and toast in a preheated 400° oven for 10 minutes, stirring halfway through. Use as a dessert topping.

walnut

NUTRIENTS

Vitamins B1, B2, B3, B5, B6, E, biotin; calcium, copper, iodine, iron, magnesium, manganese, phosphorus, potassium, selenium, zinc; fiber, protein; monounsaturated fats, omega-3 and omega-6 essential fatty acids

---

WALNUT PESTO

**a large handful of basil leaves
2 garlic cloves
20 walnuts
scant 1 cup olive oil**

Put all the ingredients in a food processor and blend until creamy. Serve stirred into wholemeal pasta or noodles, or use as a dressing for steamed vegetables.

With their two-lobed appearance resembling a brain, it's no surprise that walnuts aid cognitive function and sharpen the memory.

Walnuts are not only a good source of heart-healthy monounsaturated fats, but also contain alpha-linolenic acid, an omega-3 essential fatty acid that makes them unique among nuts. Omega-3 fats provide cardiovascular protection and aid brain function; they're also anti-inflammatory and so are useful in the treatment of asthma, rheumatoid arthritis, and skin disorders, such as eczema and psoriasis. In addition, walnuts contain the amino acid arginine, which helps to keep blood vessels flexible, and ellagic acid, an antioxidant that research has shown to have powerful anticancer properties.

coconut

Nearly every part of this health-giving tropical nut is edible, including its flesh, oil, and sap.

Although coconut is high in saturated fats, they're a different type to those found in meat and dairy and don't pose the same health risks. Known as medium chain fatty acids (MCFAs), they are easily digested and metabolized by the body, and are used as an energy source rather than being stored as fat. The coconut water—the liquid inside young coconuts—is known to be one of the most balanced electrolyte sources in nature, making a wonderful rehydration drink following intense exercise or when fluids and electrolytes have been lost through diarrhea or fever.

NUTRIENTS
Vitamins B1, B2, B3, B5, B6, C, E, folate; calcium, copper, iodine, iron, magnesium, manganese, phosphorus, potassium, selenium, zinc; fiber; protein; carbohydrate; medium chain fatty acids

NON-ALCOHOLIC PIÑA COLADA

2¼ cups pineapple juice
¾ cup coconut water
¾ cup coconut milk
8-oz. can pineapple in fruit juice

Put all the ingredients in a blender and whiz until smooth. Pour into a glass pitcher and stir well before serving with ice.

073

flaxseed

NUTRIENTS
Vitamins B1, B2, B3, B5, B6, E; calcium, copper, iron, magnesium, manganese, phosphorus, potassium, selenium, zinc; fiber; protein; omega-3 essential fatty acids

From preventing constipation to lowering high blood pressure and balancing hormones, flaxseed is truly a wonderfood.

Flaxseed (also called linseed) owes much of its healing properties to its omega-3 essential fatty acid content, which is converted in the body into hormone-like substances called prostaglandins. These are anti-inflammatory, and may benefit conditions such as asthma and arthritis. They also promote heart health by reducing cholesterol, blood pressure, and plaque formation in the artery walls. Not only this, prostaglandins encourage weight loss by removing excess fluid from tissues and boosting metabolism, thereby helping to burn calories.

A GENTLE LAXATIVE
Another great feature of flaxseed is mucilage, a type of soluble fiber that lowers cholesterol, stabilizes blood sugar levels, and alleviates constipation. Flaxseed's laxative effect is gentle, helping to keep intestinal contents moving smoothly along.

FIGHTS BREAST CANCER
The benefits of flaxseed do not stop there. This seed is also particularly rich in lignans, special compounds which are

---

PEANUT FLAX BARS

¾ cup flaxseeds
6 cups puffed rice cereal
⅓ cup crunchy peanut butter
⅓ cup brown rice syrup

Grind the flaxseeds in a coffee grinder and put them in a large bowl. Add the puffed cereal, peanut butter, and rice syrup, and mix well using your hands. Press the mixture very firmly into a nonstick baking tray and leave it for several hours before cutting into bars.

converted by friendly bacteria in the gut into two hormone-like substances called enterolactone and enterodiol. These compounds have been found to offer protection against breast cancer, as well as helping to reduce the symptoms of hot flashes during menopause.

Flaxseed also contains antiviral, antibacterial, and antifungal properties and helps to keep the skin looking youthful.

TROPICAL FLAX SHAKE

1 tbsp. flaxseeds
2½ cups pineapple juice
¾ cup apple juice
2 kiwi fruit, peeled and
  chopped
2 passion fruit, cut in half

Grind the flaxseeds in a coffee grinder and put them in a blender along with the fruit juices and kiwi fruit. Scoop out the seeds from the passion fruit and add them to the juice mixture. Blend well and drink immediately.

074

pumpkin seed

NUTRIENTS
Vitamins B2, B3, B5, E, K, beta-carotene; calcium, copper, iron, magnesium, manganese, phosphorus, potassium, zinc; fiber; protein; omega-3 and omega-6 essential fatty acids

Exciting news for men: pumpkin seeds may offer protection against prostate cancer.

Containing protein, vitamin E, and zinc (needed to heal wounds, maintain growth in children, and boost immunity), pumpkin seeds are a rich source of the essential fatty acids required for hormone balance and healthy-looking skin. These seeds are often recommended to men as a remedy for prostate enlargement, as there are components in pumpkin seed oil that interfere with prostate cell multiplication. The seeds also make an effective dewormer and have been used to help to treat roundworm, tapeworm, and other intestinal parasites.

SEEDY MUFFIN CRUNCH

3 cups flour
2 tsp. baking powder
1½ cups raisins
¾ cup pumpkin seeds
2 carrots, peeled and grated
4 cage-free eggs, beaten
¾ cup maple syrup
1 cup milk
¾ cup unrefined sunflower oil

Combine the flour, baking powder, raisins, and seeds in a bowl. Then, add the remaining ingredients and mix well to form a batter. Spoon the mixture into an oiled muffin pan and bake in a preheated 350°F oven for 20 minutes or until the muffins are a light golden color.

sesame seed

Exceptionally rich in calcium, sesame seeds are an excellent choice for nourishing the bones and teeth.

Often used to make tahini or sesame paste, these tiny seeds are packed with a broad range of minerals, including calcium, magnesium and manganese, along with generous helpings of protein and essential fatty acids. Containing 670mg of calcium per 100gm, they beat most foods, including whole milk, in the calcium stakes. In addition, sesame seeds contain a unique compound called sesamin, which has been shown to inhibit cholesterol absorption from food and prevent the development of high blood pressure.

NUTRIENTS

Vitamins B1, B2, B3, B5, B6, E, beta-carotene; calcium, copper, iodine, iron, magnesium, manganese, phosphorus, potassium, zinc; fiber; protein; omega-6 essential fatty acids

SESAME CHEWS

1⅓ cups dried dates
½ cup chopped pecans
2 tbsp. tahini
2 tbsp. peanut butter
¼ cup sesame seeds

Put 1 cup water in a pan with the dates and simmer for about 10 minutes, until soft and all the liquid has evaporated. Mash the dates and mix together with the pecans, tahini, and peanut butter. Let the mixture stand for about 30 minutes so that it firms up, then form it into small balls and coat with sesame seeds.

hemp seed

NUTRIENTS
Vitamins B1, B2, B6, C, E,
beta-carotene; calcium, copper,
iron, magnesium, manganese,
phosphorus, potassium, zinc; fibre;
protein; carbohydrate; omega-3
and omega-6 essential fatty acids,
gamma-linolenic acid

This wholesome seed contains nature's most perfectly balanced source of essential fatty acids.

Hemp seeds have an excellent balance of essential fatty acids, and include omega-3 and omega-6 in the ideal ratio for good health. These fats are converted into hormone-like substances in the body called prostaglandins which govern many important functions including growth, vitality, and mental well-being. Another important fat in hemp seeds is gamma-linolenic acid or GLA. People with eczema and other skin complaints are often deficient in this nutrient, so eating these seeds or taking hemp seed oil may be helpful in alleviating these conditions. In addition, hemp seeds contain complete protein, the quality of which is comparable to that found in meat, fish, and eggs.

HEMP SPRINKLE

3 tbsp. pumpkin seeds
3 tbsp. sunflower seeds
2 sun-dried tomatoes
½ tsp. crushed dried chilies
6 tbsp. hulled hemp seeds
1 tbsp. sesame seeds
sea salt to taste (optional)

Grind the pumpkin seeds, sunflower seeds, sun-dried tomatoes, and chilies. Put them in a bowl with the hemp seeds and sesame seeds and mix well. Add a little salt to taste if you like, and use as a sprinkle on salads and savories.

alfalfa

Eaten sprouted, alfalfa is highly regarded for its amazing array of nutrients and enzymes.

Long popular among health-food enthusiasts, alfalfa sprouts are packed with enzymes and easily digestible nutrients, which are unleashed during the sprouting process. Besides being a storehouse of amino acids, vitamins, and minerals, alfalfa contains several phytochemicals that can protect against disease. Canavanine, an amino acid analogue, exerts anti-carcinogenic activity, while the plant estrogens found in this food help to balance hormones. Other compounds abundant in alfalfa sprouts include saponins, which reduce cholesterol by binding to it so that the body can excrete it, and chlorophyll, a powerful blood-builder and detoxifying agent.

NUTRIENTS

Vitamins B3, B5, C, K, beta-carotene, folate; calcium, iron, magnesium, phosphorus, potassium, zinc; protein; enzymes

TOFU, AVOCADO, AND ALFALFA POCKETS

7 oz. smoked tofu, sliced
4 wholewheat pita breads
2 large handfuls of alfalfa sprouts
2 avocados, peeled, pitted, and sliced
2 tomatoes, sliced
12 pitted black olives, chopped
2 tbsp. tahini

Grill the tofu slices on both sides. Warm the pitas briefly in an oven, then cut them along the top and stuff with the tofu, alfalfa, avocados, tomatoes, and olives. Put the tahini and 6 tbsp. water in a bowl and mix well. Spoon over the pita filling and serve.

parsley

NUTRIENTS
Vitamins B1, B3, B5, C, E, K, beta-carotene, biotin, folate; calcium, iodine, iron, magnesium, manganese, phosphorus, potassium, selenium, zinc

The world's most popular culinary herb, there's much more to parsley than its use as a garnish.

A rich source of cancer-fighting antioxidants, including vitamin C and the flavonoid luteolin, parsley has long been used to improve arthritic and rheumatic conditions. It helps to balance fluid levels in the body by increasing potassium status and encouraging the excretion of sodium and water. This makes parsley a natural herbal diuretic and may also help to control high blood pressure. When applied topically to the skin, the herb is said to relieve irritation caused by insect bites.

PARSLEY PASTA SAUCE

2 tbsp. olive oil
½ onion, chopped
1 garlic clove, crushed
1 tsp. paprika
1¾ cups tomato puree
3 tbsp. chopped parsley
sea salt and ground black
  pepper, to taste

Heat the oil in a pan and gently fry the onion until soft. Add the garlic and paprika and continue to cook for another minute, stirring. Add the tomato puree and simmer, covered, for 20 minutes. Add the parsley and salt and pepper toward the end of cooking time. Serve over pasta.

Chewing on a parsley sprig after a meal can help to freshen the breath.

sage

Centuries-old theories about the healing properties of sage are now being proven by scientific research.

NUTRIENTS
Vitamins B3, B6, C, E, K, beta-carotene, biotin, folate; calcium, iron, magnesium, manganese, phosphorus, potassium, zinc

Not only does sage ease coughs and rheumatism, and strengthen the nervous system, but this versatile herb can also be added to gargles to relieve a sore throat and mouthwashes to combat gum inflammation. In Germany, sage has been approved for the treatment of mild gastro-intestinal complaints and excessive sweating. Thanks to its success in reducing perspiration, sage is now a popular remedy for preventing hot flashes during menopause. The herb has also been found to boost memory by increasing levels of an important chemical messenger in the brain.

MASHED POTATOES WITH SAGE

4 large potatoes, peeled and cubed
1 tbsp. butter or unhydrogenated margarine
⅓ cup soft goat cheese
2 tbsp. finely chopped sage
sea salt and ground black pepper

Steam the potatoes for about 20 minutes until soft. Transfer to a bowl, add the butter or margarine and mash well. Mix in the cheese and chopped sage, season to taste with salt and pepper, and serve.

garlic

NUTRIENTS
Vitamins B1, B3, B5, B6, C, biotin, folate; calcium, germanium, iodine, iron, magnesium, manganese, phosphorus, potassium, selenium, zinc; fiber

Garlic is a modern panacea, effective for fighting heart disease, cancer, and a host of other afflictions.

Cultivated for more than 5,000 years, garlic has been appreciated for its healing properties since the days of the ancient Egyptians. As a folk remedy, it is used in many cultures to prevent colds and flu, and in laboratory analysis it has been found to contain antibacterial, antiviral, and antifungal agents. A key active compound in garlic is allicin, which is produced from another compound, alliin, when fresh garlic is cut or crushed. Responsible for the bulb's pungent odor, this compound appears to be effective not only against common infections such as colds, flu, and candidiasis (yeast infection), but also against more hazardous microbes, such as tuberculosis, as well as the superbug MRSA (methicillin-resistant *Staphylococcus aureus*).

HEALTHY BLOOD, LOW CHOLESTEROL
Garlic has many cardiovascular benefits and its regular consumption has been proven to lower both high blood pressure and cholesterol levels. It also inhibits blood-platelet stickiness, which is associated with the formation of blood clots, and heart attacks and strokes.

GARLIC-INFUSED OLIVE OIL

1 cup extra virgin olive oil
8 garlic cloves
1 tsp. crushed chilies

Pour the oil into a large clean glass jar and add the whole garlic cloves and chilies. Secure the lid and leave it to stand in a cool, dark cupboard for several days for the flavors to develop and mingle. Use as needed for cooking or as a salad dressing.

ANTICANCER WONDER HERB

Sulfur compounds in garlic, including allicin and diallyl sulphide, appear to protect the body against cancer-forming substances and may also halt the growth of cancer cells once they develop. Ajoene, which is produced from allicin, may be useful in the treatment of skin cancer when applied topically. Other anticancer compounds in garlic include the powerful antioxidant minerals, germanium and selenium.

REFRIED BEANS

1⅓ cups dried red kidney beans
3 tbsp. olive oil
3 garlic cloves, crushed
1 tsp. chili powder
1 tsp. ground cumin
1 tsp. ground mustard seeds
1 tsp. tamari

Soak the beans in cold water overnight. Next day, drain, then put in a pan and cover with water. Bring to a boil and simmer, covered, for about 2 hours. Drain and set aside. Put the remaining ingredients with ⅓ cup water in another pan and sauté for a few minutes. Add the beans and mix well. Mash until creamy.

dill

NUTRIENTS
Vitamins B3, C, folate; calcium, iron, magnesium, phosphorus, potassium, zinc

Also known as dill weed, this herb is renowned as a treatment for digestive complaints in both adults and children.

Fresh dill makes a tangy addition to pickles, salad dressings, and fish dishes.

Dill is effective for the relief of colic, gas, and indigestion, and the active compound is thought to be an antispasmodic agent called carvone. Other components in dill have been found to indirectly neutralize cancer-forming substances, such as those in cigarette smoke and charcoal grill smoke (which may be ingested through barbecued food). Dill has also been studied for its ability to control the growth of bacteria. Taken as a tea, the herb is said to increase the production of breast milk.

NEW POTATO SALAD WITH DILL

1 lb., 10 oz. baby new
  potatoes
1 tbsp. wholegrain mustard
2 tbsp. olive oil
2 tbsp. chopped dill
sea salt and ground black
  pepper

Cut the potatoes in half and steam them for about 15 minutes until cooked through. Put them in a large bowl, add all the other ingredients, mix well, and serve.

082

mint

This herb has been treasured since ancient times for its culinary, medicinal, and aromatic properties.

The essential oil in mint is known for its ability to improve food assimilation and relieve symptoms of irritable bowel syndrome, which it does by relaxing the smooth muscles in the intestinal tract. It has also been found to inhibit the growth of several types of bacteria, including *Helicobacter pylori*—now known to be the main cause of stomach and duodenal ulcers. In addition, mint contains rosmarinic acid, an anti-inflammatory compound that encourages cells to make substances that keep the airways open for easier breathing. This may make the herb useful for respiratory disorders such as asthma.

NUTRIENTS
Vitamins B1, B2, B3, B5, B6, C, E, beta-carotene, biotin, folate; calcium, magnesium, phosphorus, potassium

MINTY YOGURT DRESSING

1⅓ cups plain live yogurt
2 tsp. finely chopped fresh basil
1 tbsp. finely chopped fresh mint
pinch of dried dill
ground black pepper, to taste

Stir all the ingredients together in a bowl and chill. This dressing is especially good on cucumber or tomato based salads, or mixed into grated root vegetables.

mustard seed

NUTRIENTS
Vitamins B1, B2, B3, B5, B6, E,
K, beta-carotene, biotin; calcium,
copper, iodine, iron, magnesium,
manganese, phosphorus,
potassium, selenium, zinc

Available in three different colors—black, brown,
and yellow—ground mustard seeds make a
flavorful addition to a range of soups, casseroles,
and curries.

A relative of broccoli and cabbage, mustard seeds contain
phytochemicals unique to this food family known as
glucosinolates. These compounds have been well studied for
their ability to stop the growth of existing cancer cells, and
to prevent new cancer cells from forming. This spice is also
an excellent source of the mineral selenium, an important
antioxidant with anti-inflammatory properties. Taken crushed,
in a little warm water, mustard seeds are believed to purify the
blood and have a mild laxative effect.

**PAN-FRIED CAULIFLOWER
WITH BEETS AND
MUSTARD SEEDS**

2 tbsp. olive oil
2 tbsp. mustard seeds
½ tsp. paprika
2 raw beets, peeled and cut
  into thin strips
1 cauliflower, broken into
  small florets
¼ cup vegetable broth

Heat the oil in a covered pan,
add the mustard seeds, cover
again, and gently fry until
they pop. Add the paprika
and vegetables and cook for
2 minutes. Add the broth and
simmer for about 8 minutes,
stirring frequently.

turmeric

This bright yellow spice has powerful properties which help to alleviate pain and inflammation.

A main spice ingredient in curries, the key active constituent in turmeric is curcumin which has been found to have a number of therapeutic actions. It reduces pain and inflammation and is commonly employed in the treatment of rheumatoid arthritis and other forms of joint pain. In fact, it may even be more effective in this area than conventional anti-inflammatory drugs. Turmeric also contains antioxidant properties, is liver-protective, and appears to prevent platelet stickiness, which may guard against heart disease and strokes.

NUTRIENTS
Vitamins B3, C, E, K, folate; calcium, iron, magnesium, manganese, phosphorus, potassium, selenium, zinc

THAI CURRY SAUCE

1¾ cups coconut milk
2 green chilies, seeded and chopped
2 garlic cloves
2 tsp. grated fresh ginger root
2 shallots, chopped
1 tbsp. olive oil
1 lemongrass stalk, peeled
1 tsp. turmeric
2 tbsp. chopped cilantro

Put the coconut milk, chilies, garlic, and ginger in a blender and whiz. Heat the oil, add the shallots, and gently fry until soft. Add the coconut mixture and the remaining ingredients. Bring to a boil and simmer for 5 minutes. Serve with rice.

ginger

NUTRIENTS
Vitamins B3, C, E, folate; calcium, iron, magnesium, phosphorus, potassium, selenium, zinc

With its soothing, pain-relieving, and anti-inflammatory properties, ginger is invaluable as a medicinal food.

Widely employed in African, Chinese, and Indian cuisines, ginger can be cooked in food to add a zingy flavor or made into a medicinal tea. But the use of ginger extends well beyond its role in the kitchen. Historically, it has been utilized for its effect on the digestive tract where it calms the stomach, dispels gas, eases nausea, and aids the absorption of nutrients.

Ginger is extremely effective as a remedy for motion or sea sickness, reducing all associated symptoms including dizziness and vomiting. It is also helpful in relieving morning sickness during pregnancy, but unlike drug-based anti-emetics that can cause harmful side effects, ginger is safe to take.

CREAMY GINGER DRESSING

¼ cup tahini
2 tsp. grated fresh ginger root
1 garlic clove
1 tsp. tamari
2 tsp. brown rice syrup

Put all the ingredients in a blender with ⅓ cup water and whiz until creamy. Serve stirred into noodles or as a salad dressing.

COMBATS ARTHRITIS
A proven treatment for osteoarthritis and rheumatoid arthritis, ginger helps to reduce pain and swelling in the joints, and improves mobility when taken on a regular basis. Its ability to work in this way has been attributed to its antioxidant properties and its potent anti-inflammatory compounds called gingerols, which suppress the substances that trigger joint inflammation.

HEART PROTECTION

Ginger supports heart health by preventing blood platelets from sticking together and lowering cholesterol levels, thereby offering protection against heart attacks and strokes. It also stimulates the circulation and is excellent for alleviating coughs and fever caused by colds or flu.

RASPBERRY GINGER WHIP

2 tsp. grated fresh ginger root
1½ cups raspberries
2 cups crème fraîche or plain
 live Greek yogurt
a handful of candied ginger,
 chopped

Put the ginger and raspberries in a food processor and blend. Add the mixture to the crème fraîche and stir. Serve chilled in individual dessert glasses, sprinkled with a few pieces of chopped candied ginger.

cinnamon

NUTRIENTS
Vitamins B2, B3, B5, B6, E, K,
beta-carotene, biotin; calcium,
copper, iodine, iron, magnesium,
manganese, phosphorus,
potassium, selenium, zinc

CINNAMON CREAM

9 oz. tofu
⅔ cup apple juice
3 tbsp. brown rice syrup
3 tbsp. unrefined sunflower oil
½ tsp. ground cinnamon

Put all the ingredients in a
food processor and blend until
smooth and creamy. Use as
a substitute for dairy cream
on desserts.

Highly prized since antiquity, cinnamon was
regarded as a gift fit for kings and it is said that
wars were even fought over it.

Used traditionally for its warming qualities, cinnamon may
help to ward off colds and improve the circulatory system. It
contains antibacterial and antifungal properties that have been
found to inhibit organisms such as *Candida albicans*, a yeast
responsible for causing candidiasis and thrush. In addition,
research has shown that compounds in cinnamon lower blood
sugar levels, which is thought to make it a promising remedy
for type 2 diabetes.

Purchase
Ceylon cinnamon,
as its flavor is
more refined than
the Indonesian
variety.

087

cardamom

Sweet and aromatic, cardamom is not only a wonderful flavoring agent but is also an antidote for a plethora of health complaints.

NUTRIENTS
Vitamins B3, C; calcium, iron, magnesium, manganese, phosphorus, potassium, zinc

Cardamom can be used whole or ground to flavor both sweet and savory dishes, and it is often made into a soothing tea. The spice stimulates the appetite and the flow of saliva, making it helpful during convalesence when the desire for food may be lacking. It can also be used to treat gum infections, sore throats, and bad breath—in India it was often employed as a gargle for this purpose. In traditional Chinese medicine, cardamom is valued as a remedy for treating stomach upsets, flatulence, and other problems of the digestive system.

HOT CARDAMOM COCOA

8 cardamom pods
4¼ cups soy milk
2 tbsp. chocolate drink powder
2 tbsp. agave syrup
1 tsp. natural vanilla extract
¼ cup grated dark chocolate
1 tsp. ground cardamom

Bruise the cardamom pods with the flat edge of a knife and put them in a saucepan. Add the soy milk, chocolate powder, agave syrup, and vanilla extract, and bring it to a boil very slowly, stirring frequently. Strain into four mugs, sprinkle with the grated chocolate and ground cardamom, and serve immediately.

egg

NUTRIENTS
Vitamins A, B2, B3, B5, B6, B12, D, E, biotin, folate; calcium, chromium, copper, iodine, iron, magnesium, manganese, phosphorus, potassium, selenium, sodium, zinc; protein; omega-3 fatty acids

Extremely versatile, eggs pack a punch on the nutritional front and are an incredible brain food.

Eggs are highly nutritious, supplying an excellent source of complete protein important for tissue repair, along with vitamins A, B12 and D, which are lacking in many foods. They also contain omega-3 fats and a B-vitamin called choline, both of which are required for normal brain function, and lutein, which can help to reduce the risk of eye disease. The nutritional value of eggs has been found to vary, with the free-range variety containing more vitamins and good fats, and less cholesterol than eggs laid by battery hens.

POTATO FRITTATA

1 lb. potatoes, peeled and chopped
1 tbsp. olive oil
4 cage-free eggs, beaten
1 tbsp. soy sauce
⅓ cup chopped parsley
ground black pepper, to taste

Steam the potatoes for 15 minutes, then transfer to the pan oiled with olive oil. Mix together the remaining ingredients and pour them over the potatoes. Cook gently 3 to 4 minutes. Once the underside is done, place under a broiler and cook until golden and set.

⊕ ⓒ ⊕ ⊙ ♡ ⊜ ⊕ ⊗

live yogurt

With its rich probiotic content, live yogurt helps to keep the digestive system in good shape by boosting the population of friendly gut bacteria.

NUTRIENTS
Vitamins A, B2, B3, B5, B12, C, D, biotin, folate; calcium, iodine, iron, magnesium, phosphorus, potassium, selenium, zinc; protein

Produced by the fermentation of milk, yogurt with live cultures contains bacteria including lactobacillus and bifido, which help to maintain levels of beneficial bacteria in the intestinal tract. Through this action, live yogurt can help to prevent constipation and alleviate the bloating, gas, and vaginal thrush often caused by an overgrowth of candida yeast. It can also avert antibiotic-related diarrhea and keep invading organisms in check, in addition to supporting the immune system.

AMBROSIA FRUIT SALAD

2 tbsp. slivered almonds
2 tbsp. flaked coconut
small can crushed pineapple, drained
1 banana, chopped
1 cup pitted cherries
⅓ cup plain live yogurt
2 tbsp. pure maple syrup
1 tsp. ground cinnamon
½ tsp. ground nutmeg

Toast the almonds and coconut in a dry pan for a few minutes, then transfer to a bowl and let cool. Add the fruit and yogurt and mix together so that all the ingredients are well combined. Spoon into individual dessert bowls, top with maple syrup, cinnamon, and nutmeg, and serve.

salmon

NUTRIENTS

Vitamins A, B1, B2, B3, B5, B6, B12, D, E, biotin, folate; calcium, iodine, iron, magnesium, phosphorus, potassium, selenium, zinc; protein; omega-3 fatty acids

BAKED SALMON WITH CAPER AND TOMATO DRESSING

4 salmon fillets
1 tbsp. capers, chopped
4 cherry tomatoes, chopped
1 shallot, chopped
1 tbsp. lemon juice
2 tbsp. olive oil

Put each salmon fillet on a piece of greased foil. Mix the remaining ingredients in a bowl and spoon them over the fillets. Fold up the foil, securing at the top to keep in juices. Place them on a baking tray and bake in a preheated 400°F oven 10 to 12 minutes until the fish is cooked. Serve.

Packed with health-giving essential fatty acids, salmon is also an excellent source of protein.

Falling into the oily fish category, salmon contains omega-3 fats in the form of eicosapentaenoic acid (EPA) and docosahexaenoic acid (DHA). These fatty acids have numerous health benefits including lowering cholesterol and high blood pressure, easing the symptoms of asthma, rheumatoid arthritis, and depression, and improving skin conditions such as eczema and psoriasis. DHA also boosts intelligence in children. In addition, salmon is a valuable source of B-vitamins and the mineral selenium, while wild salmon is rich in astaxanthin, one of the most potent antioxidants ever discovered.

turkey

Being one of the leanest forms of animal protein, this traditional festive food makes a healthier alternative to other meat and poultry.

Relatively low in fat, turkey is a superb source of protein, which the body needs for tissue growth and repair. It also contains several B-vitamins, crucial for normal metabolism and the health of the nervous system. Turkey is a rich source of anemia-preventing iron and the powerful anticancer mineral selenium, which is usually found only in small amounts in many foods. As with all meat and poultry, buying organic is the best choice, because it is likely to be lower in calories and to contain a better ratio of good to bad fats.

NUTRIENTS
Vitamins B2, B3, B5, B6, B12, D, biotin, folate; calcium, iodine, iron, magnesium, phosphorus, potassium, selenium, zinc; protein

TURKEY AND PEPPER CHIMICHANGAS

2 turkey breasts, cubed
1 red onion, chopped
1 red bell pepper, cut in strips
1 tbsp. unrefined sunflower oil
6 tbsp. store-bought salsa
4 large flour tortillas
a handful of grated cheese

Stir-fry the turkey, onion, and pepper in the oil 5 to 6 minutes. Add the salsa and heat through. Warm the tortillas in the oven and place the mixture in the center of each. Roll them up and place them seam-side down on a baking tray and top with cheese. Bake in a 350°F oven 10 to12 minutes.

🔥 🔺 ▬ 🎏

apple cider vinegar

NUTRIENTS
Vitamins B1, B2, B6, C, E, beta-carotene; calcium, chlorine, fluorine, iron, magnesium, manganese, phosphorus, potassium, selenium, silica, sulphur, zinc

It is thought that Hippocrates, the father of modern medicine, used apple cider vinegar as a healing elixir to treat his patients.

Made from the fermented juice of pressed apples, 90 different beneficial substances have been discovered in apple cider vinegar, including carbolic acids, enzymes, and trace minerals, which help to balance the body's acid–alkaline levels. Through its alkalizing effect, it is reported to alleviate a number of complaints, such as arthritis, rheumatism, headaches, heartburn, and muscle cramps. The vinegar is also used as a weight loss enhancer, which it achieves by improving fat digestion, metabolism, and liver detoxification.

FRENCH VINAIGRETTE DRESSING

3 tbsp. apple cider vinegar
⅓ cup olive oil
¼ cup unrefined sunflower oil
½ tsp. wholegrain mustard
½ tsp. paprika
½ tsp. dried mixed herbs
1 garlic clove, crushed
sea salt and ground black pepper

Place all the ingredients in a clean screwtop jar, seal, put on the lid, and shake vigorously. Store in the refrigerator for up to a week and use on salads as required.

miso

There are several types of miso available, but the darker varieties are a wise choice, as they are richer in protein and essential fatty acids.

A naturally fermented paste made from soy beans, sea salt, and koji (a yeast mold), miso is a tasty replacement for salt and adds flavor to soups, sauces, and casseroles. It's an excellent source of protein, minerals, and B-vitamins, and contains soy isoflavones—plant estrogens associated with reducing the symptoms of menopause and the risk of osteoporosis and breast cancer. It also boasts dipicolonic acid, a compound that binds to toxic metals in the body, such as mercury and lead, and removes them via the intestinal tract.

NUTRIENTS
Vitamins B1, B2, B3, B5, B6, K, beta-carotene, folate; calcium, copper, iron, magnesium, manganese, phosphorus, potassium, selenium, sodium, zinc; protein; omega-3 and omega-6 essential fatty acids

MISO SOUP

1 tbsp. sesame oil
2 scallions, trimmed and
  chopped
3½ oz smoked tofu, cut into
  small cubes
1 carrot, peeled and cut into
  matchsticks
1 tbsp. miso

Heat the oil in a pan, add the onion, tofu, and carrot, and gently fry for a few minutes until soft. Add 3¼ cups water and the miso, and simmer for 5 minutes. Serve with brown rice, noodles, or wholegrain bread.

umeboshi plum

NUTRIENTS
Vitamins B1, B2, B3; calcium, iron, phosphorus, potassium, sodium; fiber

UMEBOSHI VINAIGRETTE

½ cup sesame oil
¼ cup rice vinegar
1 tbsp. umeboshi paste
1 tsp. brown rice syrup

Put all the ingredients in a screwtop jar, seal, and shake vigorously. Keep refrigerated and use to dress salads.

This popular Japanese plum possesses a range of restorative qualities, including helping the body to recover more quickly from the effects of alcohol.

Pickled in sea salt, these tangy, tart plums are often pureed and eaten with rice. Traditionally, umeboshi plums have been used for aiding digestion and combating fatigue, actions which are thought to be linked to their alkalizing effect and ability to reduce lactic acid, a build-up of which can lead to exhaustion. In addition, the fruit's pyric acid content stimulates the function of the liver and kidneys to dissolve and expel toxins from the body, thereby enhancing the breakdown of alcohol and making these exotic plums a good remedy for hangovers.

kuzu

In addition to being a natural thickening agent, kuzu is a wonderful remedy for colds, headaches, and all kinds of digestive upsets.

Prepared from the root of a Japanese vine, kuzu's main role in the kitchen is as a thickening agent, where it adds body to soups, stews, and sauces. Besides its culinary uses, kuzu has been valued as a medicine in China and Japan for hundreds of years. It's long been a traditional remedy for warding off colds and soothing irritated mucus membranes, thereby easing intestinal pain, cramp, and diarrhea. It is also used as an alternative to aspirin for headaches, and works by altering the chemicals in the brain called neurotransmitters.

NUTRIENTS
Calcium, iron, phosphorus, potassium; carbohydrate

VEGETARIAN GRAVY

2 tbsp. kuzu
1 tbsp. olive oil
1 tsp. miso
½ tsp. vegetable bouillon
  powder
1 tsp. tamari or soy sauce

Put the kuzu and ¼ cup cold water in a bowl with and mix until dissolved. Set aside. Put the remaining ingredients in a pan with 2 cups water and bring to a boil. Reduce the heat and stir in the dissolved kuzu. Continue to stir over a low heat until the liquid begins to thicken. Serve hot or cold.

⬥ ♥ ⊕

carob

NUTRIENTS
Vitamins B1, B2, B3, B6, C, E, folate, beta-carotene; calcium, copper, iron, magnesium, manganese, phosphorus, potassium, selenium, silica, zinc; fiber; protein; carbohydrate

For anyone wishing to avoid chocolate, carob provides a tasty, caffeine-free alternative that is lower in fat and calories.

Derived from the pods of the carob tree, carob has a similar flavor to chocolate and is often used as a substitute in cakes, cookies, and desserts. The tannins in carob powder have an astringent effect on the intestines, making it useful for treating diarrhea in both adults and children. It has also shown some promise in reducing high cholesterol, thanks to its significant dietary fiber content.

FROZEN CAROB BANANAS

4 bananas
4 wooden sticks
7 oz. bar of carob
½ cup crushed nuts

Peel the bananas and cut them in half. Insert a wooden stick into the flat end of each banana half, put them on a lined tray, and freeze them for about 2 hours. Melt the carob in a double boiler, then dip each banana into the carob and coat well. Finally, roll them in nuts and refreeze. Serve frozen.

Unlike chocolate, which is toxic to most animals, carob-based treats are considered safe for pets.

dark chocolate

Craved more than any other food in the world, chocolate—mainly the dark variety—delivers several health benefits.

Chocolate lovers can delight in the knowledge that their favorite treat is good for them. Studies have shown that dark chocolate, which has a high cocoa content, contains epicatechin and gallic acid, antioxidants with heart-protective properties. These compounds may have anticancer activity, too. Chocolate also possesses phenylethylamine, an amphetamine-like compound that acts as a natural mood enhancer, and theobromine, which is a mild stimulant. To reap the benefits of dark chocolate, it should be eaten regularly in small amounts.

NUTRIENTS
Vitamins B3, B5, E, beta-carotene, biotin, folate; calcium, copper, iron, iodine, magnesium, manganese, phosphorus, potassium, selenium, zinc; fiber; protein; carbohydrate

CHOCOLATE MARZIPAN

1¾ cups ground almonds
¼ cup brown rice syrup
1 tbsp. natural almond
  extract
½ cup dark chocolate

Mix together the ground almonds, brown rice syrup, and almond extract to form a thick paste. Using your hands, roll the mixture into small balls (should make about 14) and set aside. Break the chocolate into pieces and melt it in a double boiler. Dip the balls in the melted chocolate, place them on a lined tray, and let them set.

honey

Besides being a natural sweetener, honey has many wonderful properties, including substances that speed up wound healing and fight superbugs.

Produced by bees from flower nectar, honey is the most natural of all sweeteners and is a viable replacement for sugar. As an energy source, it enhances sports performance by providing a welcome boost both during and after exercise. No wonder honey is considered a general pick-me-up!

ANTIOXIDANT POWER
Containing small amounts of vitamins, minerals, and amino acids, honey appears to improve the status of protective antioxidants in the blood when consumed on a regular basis. In addition, a spoonful of honey with lemon in hot water can also soothe a sore throat and help to ease the symptoms of coughs and colds.

SUPERBUG SUPER-FIGHTER
There is a specific type of New Zealand honey called Manuka, which has been found to have powerful antibiotic properties. These inhibit the growth of bacteria, including *Helicobacter pylori*, which is associated with causing most stomach and

NUTRIENTS
Vitamins B3, B5, B6, biotin, folate; calcium, magnesium, manganese, iron, phosphorus, potassium, selenium, zinc; carbohydrate

HONEY ALMOND CUP

2 cups rice milk
1½ cups almonds
2 tbsp. honey
1 tbsp. natural vanilla extract

Put the rice milk and almonds in a blender with 1¼ cups water and mix well. Pour the liquid through a strainer into a glass pitcher. Stir in the honey and vanilla extract, then chill in the fridge. Serve.

duodenal ulcers. The antibacterial activity of this honey is also proving to be an effective weapon in combating superbugs, such as MRSA (Methicillin-resistant *Staphylococcus aureus*), strains of which have become particularly resistant to conventional antibiotic treatment.

Manuka honey can also be used topically in the healing of skin ulcers, wounds, boils, and burns, where it reduces inflammation and promotes tissue regeneration. Moreover, because it also has potent antifungal properties, this special honey has been used effectively to treat athlete's foot and other fungal infections.

BANANA, HONEY, AND NUT BAGELS

4 wholegrain bagels
heaping ⅓ cup crunchy peanut butter
4 bananas, chopped
heaping 1 tbsp. honey
½ tsp. ground cinnamon

Cut the bagels in half and spread with peanut butter. Mash the bananas and mix them with the honey and cinnamon, then spoon the mixture on top of the peanut butter. Broil the bagels for a few minutes and serve immediately.

blackstrap molasses

This thick, dark, sticky syrup helps nourish red blood cells and boost flagging energy levels.

A by-product of the sugar cane refining process, this nutritious sweetener imparts a robust, bittersweet flavor and can be added to cookies, tomato sauces, and homemade baked beans. Often recommended as a remedy for anemia, just two teaspoons of blackstrap molasses provide around a quarter of an adult's daily iron needs. It is a good source of other minerals, such as calcium, which is needed for bone maintenance, and manganese, which plays a role in nerve health. It can also be taken as a supplement to improve general nutrient status.

BOSTON BAKED BEANS

1 cup dried navy beans
1 tsp. garlic powder
1 tsp. ground mustard
2 tbsp. olive oil
1 tsp. dried oregano
2 tbsp. tomato paste
3 bay leaves
2 tsp. blackstrap or dark
    molasses

Soak the beans overnight in cold water. Next day, drain, and place in a pan with water. Bring to a boil and simmer for 2 hours. Drain and set aside. Sauté the garlic and mustard in the oil. Add all the remaining ingredients and 2 cups water, and simmer, covered, for 15 minutes.

xylitol

Xylitol looks and tastes just like white sugar, but rather than encouraging dental caries, it has been found actually to reduce tooth decay.

Extracted from the wood fiber of birch trees, xylitol is a type of carbohydrate that can be used spoon for spoon instead of sugar in drinks, desserts and baking. However, because it has a very low glycaemic index, it's suitable for diabetics and those with poor blood sugar balance. Unlike other sweeteners, xylitol inhibits the development of tooth decay by reducing the secretion of plaque acids, especially in people who use xylitol-containing chewing gum or toothpaste on a regular basis.

NUTRIENTS
Carbohydrate

CAROB BROWNIES

scant 1 cup unhydrogenated margarine
½ cup xylitol
1½ cups rice flour
¼ cup carob powder
2 tbsp. arrowroot powder
1 tsp. baking powder
a handful of chopped walnuts
scant 1 cup rice milk
1 tbsp. natural vanilla extract

Cream together the margarine and xylitol, then add the rice flour, carob, arrowroot, and baking powder, and mix. Add the remaining ingredients and mix well. Spoon into an oiled baking tray, spread evenly, and bake in a preheated 350°F oven for 30 minutes.

ailments directory

ANEMIA

watercress (p.25), Jerusalem artichoke (p.35), kombu (p.44), nori (p.46), dulse (p.48), quinoa (p.79), amaranth (p.80), chickpea (p.83), lentil (p.84), alfalfa (p.95), turkey (p.111), blackstrap molasses (p.120).

ARTHRITIS

celery (p.16), radicchio (p.23), olive and olive oil (p.29), kombu (p.44), cherry (p.54), raspberry (p.61), goji berry (p.62), açai berry (p.63), pomegranate (p.68), papaya (p.71), pineapple (p.72), millet (p.78), walnut (p.88), flaxseed (p.90), parsley (p.96), turmeric (p.103), ginger (p.104), salmon (p.110), apple cider vinegar (p.112), kuzu (p.115).

ASTHMA

fennel (p.15), radicchio (p.23), sweet potato (p.39), butternut squash (p.42), nori (p.46), raspberry (p.61), açai berry (p.63), walnut (p.88), flaxseed (p.90), mint (p.101), salmon (p.110).

CANCER

cucumber (p.12), tomato (p.13), red pepper (p.14), fennel (p.15), celery (p.16), leek (p.18), eggplant (p.19), asparagus (p.20), artichoke (p.21), lettuce (p.22), radicchio (p.23), spinach (p.24), watercress (p.25), shiitake mushroom (p.27), olive and olive oil (p.29), cabbage (p.30), broccoli (p.32), carrot (p.33), beet (p.34), Jerusalem artichoke (p.35), mooli (p.36), potato (p.38), sweet potato (p.39), yam (p.40), butternut squash (p.42), kombu (p.44), hijiki (p.49), apple (p.50), grape (p.53), prune (p.58), blueberry (p.59), cranberry (p.60), raspberry (p.61), goji berry (p.62), açai berry (p.63), tangerine (p.64), grapefruit (p.65), lemon (p.66), pomegranate (p.68), oats (p.74), almond (p.86), walnut (p.88), flaxseed (p.90), alfalfa (p.95), garlic (p.98), dill (p.100), mustard seed (p.102), turmeric (p.103), turkey (p.111), miso (p.113), dark chocolate (p.117).

CANDIDIASIS

garlic (p.98), ginger (p.104), cinnamon (p.106), live yogurt (p.109).

COMMON COLD

tomato (p.13), red pepper (p.14), eggplant (p.19), lettuce (p.22), watercress (p.25), shiitake mushroom (p.27), broccoli (p.32), carrot (p.33), potato (p.38), sweet potato (p.39), horseradish (p.41), nori (p.46), blueberry (p.59), raspberry (p.61), goji berry (p.62), tangerine (p.64), grapefruit (p.65), lemon (p.66), guava (p.67), pomegranate (p.68), garlic (p.98), ginger (p.104), cinnamon (p.106), kuzu (p.115), honey (p.118).

CONSTIPATION

artichoke (p.21), okra (p.26), cabbage (p.30), beet (p.34), agar-agar (p.43), apple (p.50), pear (p.51), grape (p.53), fig (p.57), prune (p.58), raspberry (p.61), açai berry (p.63), grapefruit (p.65), kiwi fruit (p.70), oats (p.74), barley (p.75),

brown rice (p.76), millet (p.78), quinoa (p.79), amaranth (p.80), buckwheat (p.81), chickpea (p.83), lentil (p.84), flaxseed (p.90), mustard seed (p.102), live yogurt (p.109).

COUGHS

carrot (p.33), horseradish (p.41), lemon (p.66), sage (p.97), ginger (p.104), honey (p.118).

DEPRESSION (MILD)

banana (p.52), goji berry (p.62), brown rice (p.76), almond (p.86), walnut (p.88), egg (p.108), salmon (p.110), dark chocolate (p.117).

DIABETES

leek (p.18), okra (p.26), shiitake mushroom (p.27), avocado (p.28), Jerusalem artichoke (p.35), sweet potato (p.39), yam (p.40), hijiki (p.49), blueberry (p.59),

guava (p.67), oats (p.74), barley (p.75), brown rice (p.76), millet (p.78), quinoa (p.79), amaranth (p.80), buckwheat (p.81), chickpea (p.83), lentil (p.84), cinnamon (p.106), turkey (p.111), xylitol (p.121).

DIARRHEA

banana (p.52), date (p.56), guava (p.67), barley (p.75), coconut (p.89), live yogurt (p.109), kuzu (p.115), carob (p.116).

EYE DISEASE

asparagus (p.20), spinach (p.24), watercress (p.25), broccoli (p.32), carrot (p.33), nori (p.46), blueberry (p.59), goji berry (p.62), kiwi fruit (p.70), egg (p.108).

FATIGUE

cucumber (p.12), celery (p.16), shiitake mushroom (p.27),

taro (p.37), potato (p.38), sweet potato (p.39), yam (p.40), butternut squash (p.42), banana (p.52), date (p.56), prune (p.58), oats (p.74), barley (p.75), brown rice (p.76), millet (p.78), quinoa (p.79), amaranth (p.80), buckwheat (p.81), chickpea (p.83), lentil (p.84), coconut (p.89), umeboshi plum (p.114), dark chocolate (p.117), honey (p.118), blackstrap molasses (p.120).

GUM INFLAMMATION

cranberry (p.60), pomegranate (p.68), sage (p.97), cardamom (p.107), live yogurt (p.109), xylitol (p.121).

HEART DISEASE

tomato (p.13), fennel (p.15), celery (p.16), leek (p.18), asparagus (p.20), artichoke (p.21), spinach (p.24),

watercress (p.25), okra (p.26), shiitake mushroom (p.27), avocado (p.28), olive and olive oil (p.29), carrot (p.33), agar-agar (p.43), wakame (p.47), hijiki (p.49), apple (p.50), pear (p.51), grape (p.53), blueberry (p.59), raspberry (p.61), açai berry (p.63), tangerine (p.64), grapefruit (p.65), pomegranate (p.68), kiwi fruit (p.70), persimmon (p.73), oats (p.74), barley (p.75), brown rice (p.76), millet (p.78), quinoa (p.79), amaranth (p.80), buckwheat (p.81), chickpea (p.83), lentil (p.84), soy bean (p.85), almond (p.86), macadamia nut (p.87), walnut (p.88), flaxseed (p.90), sesame seed (p.93), hemp seed (p.94), garlic (p.98), turmeric (p.103), ginger (p.104), salmon (p.110), carob (p.116), dark chocolate (p.117).

HIGH BLOOD PRESSURE

celery (p.16), leek (p.18), shiitake mushroom (p.27), olive and olive oil (p.29), potato (p.38), kombu (p.44), wakame (p.47), dulse (p.48), banana (p.52), grape (p.53), açai berry (p.63), pomegranate (p.68), amaranth (p.80), buckwheat (p.81), flaxseed (p.90), sesame seed (p.93), hemp seed (p.94), parsley (p.96), garlic (p.98), salmon (p.110).

INDIGESTION

artichoke (p.21), radicchio (p.23), taro (p.36), horseradish (p.41), kombu (p.44), papaya (p.71), pineapple (p.72), mint (p.101), ginger (p.104), live yogurt (p.109), apple cider vinegar (p.112), umeboshi plum (p.114).

INFLUENZA

red bell pepper (p.14),

eggplant (p.19), lettuce (p.22), watercress (p.25), shiitake mushroom (p.27), broccoli (p.32), horseradish (p.41), blueberry (p.59), raspberry (p.61), goji berry(p.62), tangerine (p.64), grapefruit (p.65), lemon (p.66), pomegranate (p.68), garlic (p.98), ginger (p.104), honey (p.118).

IRRITABLE BOWEL SYNDROME

fennel (p.15), artichoke (p.21), okra (p.26), brown rice (p.76), millet (p.78), flaxseed (p.90), dill (p.100), mint (p.101), ginger (p.104), cardamom (p.107), live yogurt (p.109), kuzu (p.115).

MENOPAUSE

fennel (p.15), soy bean (p.85), flaxseed (p.90), alfalfa (p.95), sage (p.97), miso (p.113).

OSTEOPOROSIS

spinach (p.24), watercress (p.25), broccoli (p.32), kombu (p.44), nori (p.46), wakame (p.47), hijiki (p.49), fig (p.57), pineapple (p.72), quinoa (p.79), amaranth (p.80), soy bean (p.85), sesame seed (p.93), live yogurt (p.109), miso (p.113).

RHEUMATISM

celery (p.16), kombu (p.44), cherry (p.54), millet (p.78), parsley (p.96), sage (p.97), ginger (p.104), apple cider vinegar (p.112).

SKIN COMPLAINTS

cucumber (p.12), tomato (p.13), avocado (p.28), olive and olive oil (p.29), carrot (p.33), wakame (p.47), açai berry (p.63), guava (p.67), papaya (p.71), walnut (p.88), flaxseed (p.90), pumpkin

seed (p.92), hemp seed (p.94), salmon (p.110).

UNDER-ACTIVE THYROID

kombu (p.44), nori (p.46), wakame (p.47), dulse (p.48), hijiki (p.49).

URINARY TRACT INFECTIONS

horseradish (p.41), blueberry (p.59), cranberry (p.60), raspberry (p.61), barley (p.75), aduki bean (p.82), garlic (p.98).

WATER RETENTION

cucumber (p.12), tomato (p.13), celery (p.16), asparagus (p.20), lettuce (p.22), Jerusalem artichoke (p.35), taro (p.37), potato (p.38), sweet potato (p.39), yam (p.40), horseradish (p.41), banana (p.52), date (p.56), barley (p.75), aduki bean (p.82), parsley (p.96).

glossary

Alginic acid A polysaccharide in various sea vegetables that has the ability to remove heavy metals from the body.

Allicin A compound in garlic that has potent antibacterial and antifungal activities.

Anthocyanins Colorful pigments found in various fruit and vegetables, which are powerful antioxidants.

Antioxidants Compounds abundant in fruit and vegetables that inhibit the effects of damaging free radicals.

Beta-cryptoxanthin A carotenoid compound with antioxidant activity found in winter squash, papaya, and watermelon.

Beta-glucan Soluble fiber with many health-giving attributes found in barley and oats.

Beta-sitosterol A phytosterol compound found in many natural foods that lowers cholesterol.

Bromelain An enzyme in pineapple that aids protein digestion and has anti-inflammatory effects.

Caffeic acid An antioxidant compound in many fruits, vegetables, and herbs.

Calcium pectate A type of fiber that adds crispness to fruits and vegetables, and has powerful cholesterol-lowering properties.

Carotenoids Colored pigments in various fruit and vegetables, which function as antioxidants. Some of them are converted in the body into vitamin A.

Carvone A natural anti-spasmodic agent found in the oils of dill and caraway seed.

Diallyl sulphide A sulfur compound with anticancer activity found in garlic.

Diindolylmethane A compound found in broccoli and other cruciferous vegetables, which

has anticancer, antiviral, and antibacterial properties.

Electrolyte A substance containing free ions, such as sodium, potassium, calcium, magnesium, and chloride.

Ellagic acid A polyphenol antioxidant with anticancer properties found in many fruit and vegetables.

Flavonoids An umbrella term for a class of antioxidants found in many natural foods.

Free radicals Highly reactive molecules linked to causing degenerative diseases and the aging process.

Fucoidan A polysaccharide in various sea vegetables that appears to destroy cancer cells.

Glucosinolates Compounds that have anticancer activity, found in broccoli, cabbage, brussels sprouts, mustard seeds, and other Brassicaceae.

Hesperidin A flavonoid antioxidant in citrus fruit that has anticancer and heart-protective properties.

Homocysteine An amino acid in the blood, high levels of which are linked to an increased risk of heart disease and stroke.

Inulin A type of carbohydrate that does not elevate blood sugar levels and so may help in the management of diabetes.

Isoflavones Phyto-estrogen compounds found in soy and other foods that have estrogen-like actions in the body.

Kaempferol A flavonoid antioxidant in fennel, broccoli, grapefruit, and other plant-derived sources.

Limonene A cancer-fighting compound in citrus fruit.

Lutein An antioxidant carotenoid associated with eye health.

Lycopene An antioxidant carotenoid found in red foods, such as tomatoes, that has anticancer activity.

Melatonin A potent antioxidant produced by the body's pineal gland that helps to regulate sleep patterns.

Pectin A type of soluble fiber in fruit and vegetables that lowers cholesterol levels.

Phenylethylamine A natural mood-enhancing chemical found in chocolate.

Phytochemical Natural plant compounds abundant in fruit and vegetables that possess antioxidant activity.

Phytosterols Plant compounds that help to lower high cholesterol levels.

Proanthocyanidins A class of flavonoids with antioxidant activity found in various berries. They also help with skin maintenance and strengthen blood vessels.

Pterostilbene A compound present in blueberries and grapes, which has anticancer and cholesterol-lowering properties and is thought to reduce cognitive decline.

Quercetin An anti-inflammatory flavonoid that is particularly abundant in capers, apples, and onions.

Resveratrol An antioxidant found in grapes and blueberries that has anticancer, anti-inflammatory, and antiviral properties.

Rutin A flavonoid antioxidant that helps to strengthen the blood vessels.

Squalene A compound found in amaranth seed, rice bran, wheat germ, and olives that can help to reduce high blood pressure and elevated cholesterol levels.

Sulforaphane A cancer-fighting compound that can be obtained by eating cruciferous vegetables such as broccoli, brussels sprouts, and cabbage.

Tangeritin A cholesterol-lowering antioxidant found in tangerines and other citrus fruit.

Zeaxanthin An antioxidant carotenoid associated with eye health.

index